Boyhood Memories o
In Nineteen Forties Great St

By John Lovell

Being inspired and encouraged by Mrs. Margaret Faulkner, a well known and appreciated local writer, whose name will obviously crop up again in these memories, I too decided to write about my childhood.

I strongly recommend that you read Margaret's

A VILLAGE CHILDHOOD
There will be some overlapping of memories as we are of the same age, and from the same village and were childhood sweethearts when we were about nine or ten years old.

Bright Pen

Visit us online at www.authorsonline.co.uk

A Bright Pen Book

Copyright John Lovell © 2011

Cover design by John Lovell, Richard and James Fitt ©

All rights reserved. No part of this publication may be reproduced, stored in a retrieval system, or transmitted in any form or by any means, electronic, mechanical, photocopy, recording or otherwise, without prior written permission of the copyright owner. Nor can it be circulated in any form of binding or cover other than that in which it is published and without similar condition including this condition being imposed on a subsequent purchaser.

ISBN 978 0 7552 1308 5

Authors On Line Ltd
19 The Cinques
Gamlingay, Sandy
Bedfordshire SG19 3NU
England

This book is also available in e-book format, details of which are available at www.authorsonline.co.uk

Forward

This book has been compiled from my memories as I recall them, and not in any exact order, but as I saw the world at that time. In the nineteen forties and fifties from childhood to teenager

Any poor compilation is completely of my own doing and no blame for this should not be laid at anyone else's door. This is my story as I have written it.

Many of the people in this story have been long gone, but the memories, affectionate or not, still remain and as I remember it a happy time.

Acknowledgments

I would like to thank Dr. Richard Halliday for the loan of his material on The Hall at Great Stukeley and The Park By reading this I was able to confirm that my memories were correct and that I could confidently put them into print.

Thanks to Huntingdon Library for reproducing copies of local maps to confirm my memories of certain locations.

A very special word of thanks to Margaret Faulkener for the encouragement and advice given to me to create this book, as without her help I may never have started it.

I would like to thank The Goodlif Committee (Huntingdon Local History Society), for their generosity in helping me to finance this project, without their help I would not have been able to start this book.

I dedicate this book to my parents, Verena and Arthur, who are no longer with us. My Father having died long ago at the age of just fifty, my Mother more recently at the age of ninety two.

I thank them for bringing me up to live a good and honest life.

And finally my dear wife Ann, who on taking over from my parents, has kept me on the straight and narrow for the past fifty five years. And putting up with my pondering over my memories, and tip tapping on my keyboard.

Contents

A Short Rundown of My Family	9
The Village and its People, as I remember them from an early age	18
Early Days	34
The War Years	38
Aerodromes and Aircraft	66
On The Farm	79
Home Grown	111
Great Stukeley Hall and Park	123
Working in My School Years	139
'Odds And Ends'	151
Mothers Hair.	152
The Wicksteed Park Saga.	152
Snowed In	153
Developing Stukeley.	155
Surprise Visit.	156
Vic Clarks Rabbits	158
Places of Interest.	160

Illustrations

My Mother at about nineteen years old	11
My Father as a young man at Lodge farm	12
Father as a young man at Lodge Farm front door	13
Father with younger sister at 'The Lodge'	14
Grandfather with Father's older sister Mable at 'The Lodge'	14
My first portrait taken by Mr Earnest Whitney,	15
Me at six months, winning a baby show at Abbots Ripon. The prize was a 'Chad Valley' pink elephant, which I still own	15
Jean Hamilton and Russell Hobbs teaching me to walk	16
Walking on my own at about one year old at the back of our cottage in Green End	16
A Donkey ride at Hunstanton with Audry (Pansy) and Freddy (Nip) Peacock from Abbots Rippon, family friends	17
My and my auntie Marjory (Mother's younger sister) on the stile opposite our house	17
On my bike in Green End, showing Mr Juggins' Washingly Farm in the background	23
On my bike in my 'smart suit' showing the old railway carriage in the background, which had been made into a bungalow	23
This is the Horsehoes Restaurant at the top of Church Road. When I was a boy it was the Farm House and Cottage	29
This is the Old School House, at the end of what is known as Church End, where Miss Leppard lived until she retired	31
Mother and Father with Mrs Perry, Pauline and me	39

Pauline with me on my bike   39

Mother and Father (in his Home Guard uniform) with George and I
                                                                   40

School photo of me with my 'Coy' look   41

Another picture showing my first fountain pen bought for me by George's parents we both had the same type of pen. They were 'Mentmore' pens, collectable now   41

Our old house at Green End   49

Mother and father about 1939/40 at back of the old house   50

My Grandfather taking a break in the harvest field. He is well into his late seventies and still working full time   60

Ladies in the harvest field. Left to right: Mother, Mrs Gough, Mrs Wendholt (Wendy), Ida Bates and Kate Byford   60

This is a 'potato spinner', when the leading blade has passed under the crop the two spinning tines that turn inwards leave the potatoes in a row ready to pick up   61

Sugarbeet waiting to be picked up, at the top end of Green End 87

(Standard) Fordson Tractor. Several models of this were made over the years, quite a few coming to Grange farm   90

Bottom: Fordson (Major), its doesn't look too bad here but when the first one was delivered to The Grange with iron wheels everyone though how ugly compared to the old Standard model 90

The International Harvester Co. 'T6' Tractor. It had a petrol/paraffin engine, not diesel. This was the first 'Crawler' type used at Grange farm   91

A 'Fowler Marshall' the type driven by Jimmy Lightfoot   92

The little grey 'Ferguson' used by my father when he looked after the cattle   92

A Titan tractor. The first tractor my father drove. First introduced into the country in about 1919 and already on Grange Farm   93

A Hay Sweep mounted on a tractor Not on the old Buick motor that I can remember   101

This is the type of tractor and plough my father let me drive on my own   102

A reaper similar to the one at Grange farm   103

A pair of steam 'Ploughing Engines' similar to the type that used to visit Grange Farm. Note the cable drum on the underside   106

Sitting on Mr. Deller's fence with my bandaged ankle after the farm dog had bitten me.   110

School picture with my Cub's neckerchief   110

A picture of The Hall grounds as date shown. This looked out from the terrace and into the park towards Green End. You can see the boundary (ha-ha!) showing between the trees   124

At Stukely Hall in the 1870s the Tillards gave employment to these 18 people photographed outside the coach house. The coach house has been given a new lease of life as a private residence.   125

A 'Farmall' tractor made by the International Harvester Co. USA. This is the type we had on Mr Juggins' farm, the one that Jim Hayes was driving when the wheel came off!   142

John Deer Model 'H' tractor as used at Grange Farm_also on Mr Juggins' farm   143

A 'Binder' that cut the standing crop, tied it into bundles and dropped in rows ready to be picked up and carted off.   144

A John Deere model 'B' Mr Juggins' second tractor, his other one was a model 'H' like the one at Grange farm   144

Later model of the 'Standard' Fordson tractor   145

A Short Rundown of My Family

I was born on the 16th of March 1934 at Lodge Farm Great Stukeley, which belonged to Mr. Josh Gifford, the grand father of the well known horse trainer of the same name.

Lodge farm was on the (Abbots Ripton) side of the railway but in Great Stukeley parish.

My parents didn't reside at the farm at that time, they were there only for my Mothers confinement. They had a small cottage in Green End in the village. My grandparents lived in the farm house along with my Father's two brothers and two sisters who were living at home.

The Lodge Farm house was a really large house, in two sections, though all one at one time no doubt. It is 'T' shaped the long tail end being of less quality, with smaller rooms and stone floors. The Posh end where Grandfather lived had much larger rooms with higher ceilings and boarded floors.

People named Buddle lived in the other half when Grandfather moved in

My Grandfather a Fenman had moved up to what was known as 'the high land' to be foreman horse keeper for the Gifford family, when my father was about sixteen. I didn't know my Grandparents on my Mothers side, as they had both died at an early age, when my Mother was sixteen; she was the eldest of four children. They lived at Wild Goose Leys Farm in Abbots Ripton, only a stones throw from Lodge Farm. That was how my parents became teenage sweethearts.

My father was a keen sportsman, involved cricket, football and boxing. When he was a teenager living in Chatteris Fen he would cycle into Chatteris and be 'striker,' that is using a hammer for the blacksmith, who was Mr. Boon. He had a young son Eric, who become famous as a professional boxer, and was British champion at one time. My father carried on with this for some time after moving to lodge farm, some ride just to keep fit, not that working on the farm didn't do this, but also to build up some sort of physique. My father became a sparring partner for a local boxer, Con Bird of Abbots Ripton, who would have turned professional, but at that time opportunities were not as they are today.

Father played football for Brampton for several seasons. They were rated as a good local team. Only giving up when I was born. His good friend Charlie Deller[1], played for the same team. As soon as there was a Stukeley cricket or football team, both Father and Charlie were in like a flash.

---

[1] As you will see the name 'Deller' appears several times, which I have commented on early in these memories. Since compiling this book I have come across an old newspaper cutting sent to my mother by Roy Hobbs some years ago. It is a photograph of the children at Great Stukeley School in 1932. This is before Miss Leppard's time. There were 31 children age between 7 & 14 and there are no less than 9 Dellers. When I was at the same school between 1939 and 1949 I can recall 6 in my age group.

My Mother at about nineteen years old

My Father as a young man at Lodge farm
Note the Carbide Gas Lamp

Father as a young man at Lodge Farm front door

Father with younger sister at 'The Lodge'

Grandfather with Father's older sister Mable at 'The Lodge'

*My first portrait taken by Mr Earnest Whitney,
the well known Huntingdon photographer*

Me at six months, winning a baby show at Abbots Ripon. The prize was a 'Chad Valley' pink elephant, which I still own

Jean Hamilton and Russell Hobbs teaching me to walk

Walking on my own at about one year old at the back of our cottage in Green End

Top: *A Donkey ride at Hunstanton with Audry (Pansy) and Freddy (Nip) Peacock from Abbots Rippon, family friends*

Right: *By the river with Mother and Pansy Peacock. Note the same hat*

Bottom: *Me and my auntie Marjory (Mother's younger sister) on the stile opposite our house*

17

The Village and its People, as I remember them from an early age

After leaving Huntingdon, on the left hand side on the approach to the village there is the road to Brookfield Farm, owned and farmed by Harry Raby. He had three sons. Harry, George and Sam. Young Harry now farms Brookfield. George and Sam have farms at other locations. There are about four cottages with the farm, two of which can be seen from the main road. One of these was occupied by one of the many families of Deller living in the village at this time. There were about twelve children in that family. I can't recall all of them, as only the youngest one is of my age, that being Tony. Those I remember are Flossie, Jessie and Freda, all the others were older so there was only occasional contact, when I visited Tony for play.

The next house on the left was that of Mr. &. Mrs. Molecaster, Mr. Molecaster was a director of Messrs Yarnold's Garage and Yarnolds Bookmakers. This house is now the home of the Rt. Hon John Major.

On the right hand side is Green End. Starting with the 'Blacksmiths Shop' This used to be a fork road, but the approach from north side has been long closed. I can just remember the old forge being there, but it was not in use. On the end of the building there as a small bill board, which used to advertise the forth coming events for the Hippordrome cinema in Huntingdon. The owners of the Blacksmiths were Mr. & Mrs. Owen and they lived in the house adjacent. Because of having the bill board, Mrs. Owen had two complementary tickets for the cinema each week, which she often gave to her friends. Mr. Owen had a small tipper lorry business, mostly contracting to the local council and some sugar-beet carting, later adding a second lorry. Mr. and Mrs. Owen were quite a bit older than my parents. I remember Mr. Owen as being slightly bent forward, and having quite large feet. Mrs Owen was a rather well built lady, being large busted and always on the go. She took in washing for the Americans off the Alconbury base. I think she did the washing for about six men, there were what seemed to be endless lines of washing across their large yard. It was alleged that she rather liked her Guinness and would have four or five bottles before starting her washing, at about six o-clock in the morning. In the yard was a big black barn raised up off the ground and children could hide underneath this, also in the yard was a big walnut tree which yielded huge amounts of nuts, my mother use to buy some of these when they were still green for pickling, these were delicious.

The old house has gone now and a new one was built when the Gilson family owned the property. It is now owned by a Mr. Helm who is a thatcher.

Mr.& Mrs. Owen retired to a cottage in Huntingdon, on the corner of the main road and Great Northen Street, an area known as 'Toby's Trunk.'

The next house is on the right hand side, was owned by Mr. Harold Thackray, he was the owner of F.B Thackray Builders Huntingdon. Mr.& Mrs. Thackray had three sons, John, Roger and Edward, all younger than me. Sadly Roger died at about fourteen..

Next were a row of four cottages, on the left hand side of the road. In the first one lived Mr.& Mrs. Robinson and their daughter Kate, she was about my parents age who became Mrs. Byford. The second cottage is where I lived until I was about fourteen months old, when we moved up the road a little, and Mr.& Mrs. Hayward moved in. They had a son Basil who served in the navy during the war. Mrs. Hayward had a large Macaw, who squawked a lot but I don't remember if he talked. Mrs. Hayward was an Irish lady and she had a saying that has stuck with me which was ' I like me bread tin and me butter tick' Mr. Hayward worked on the council, he was what was known as a 'length man' which meant that he was responsible for keeping the road tidy removing all debris that may be found its way on the road, keeping the gutters free and all general maintenance which could be carried out by hand.

Next door was Mr. & Mrs. Hobbs who had four grown up sons, all who served in the forces during the War. Mr. Dick Hobbs worked at Grange Farm, where he was the engine driver. The farm had their own steam engine, which was used to drive the threshing machine. Mrs. Hobbs took two nephews under her wing Albert and Ronald Jacobs, who were orphaned. And in the last one lived Mr.&. Mrs. Hamilton with their two children, Jean and Charlie, who were both quite a bit older than me. Mr. Hamilton was the stoker at Castle Hill House Council Offices, looking after the boilers. He was in the navy as a young man as was Charlie when he was old enough.

Across the road was a single house where Mr. Henson lived with a spinster lady, Miss Sophie Fogle, she was his niece, and I have been told that she had a lot to do with teaching me to walk, which apparently I was quite proficient at about ten months old. Next across to the left side was a single house, where lived Granny Green and three of her grown up children, who were my parents age. There was George, Bill, who was a Policeman and Gussie. There were two other married daughters. One to Mr. Essey Prior, (obviously this was not his real name!) Her name was Eva and the other one was married to a Mr. Tom Young, who was a butcher and they lived in London.

Next was the house where I lived until I married, apart from two years National Service. Our house was part of an older building that had been much larger and made into two at sometime, with a small cottage joined on round the corner at right angles to rear of the part next to us. We lived in the left hand side, facing the front, the cottage couldn't be seen from the road. Both the cottage and the other part of the main building changed residents several times in my childhood. Then there was an old railway carriage, which had been converted into a type of bungalow, also changing residents several times. These dwellings belonged to Grange Farm.

Across the road were two thatched cottages joined together, they may also have been one in previous years, probably seventeenth century.

In the first one Mr.&. Mrs. Charles Deller lived with their son Charlie and daughter Olive who became Mrs. Reg Cade. Charlie was my fathers age, a life long friend and workmate. Mr. Deller senior had a small holding with some nice buildings, including a big black barn and buildings for cattle etc. He had a small horse and a flat bed four wheeled wagon, with which he used to take his produce to Huntingdon, always walking with his horse never riding. He also had an orchard with, amongst other things, some beautiful Victoria plum, as big as hen's eggs, much bigger than they are nowadays and they tasted all the better when they were scrumped. In the other cottage lived Mr.&. Mrs. Wilson and their son Jeffery who was quite a bit older than me, so we didn't have much contact. I remember Mr. Wilson kept bees and sometime we were treated to the odd jar of honey. People seemed more friendly and neighbourly in those days. Probably because they didn't move around as much then, and all knew each other much longer, and most likely all their business as well.

Mr. Wilson worked for the county council, mainly on road maintenance I think. One would often see him with the white lining machine with just a red flag tied round his waist for ' protection?' No cones in those days.

The next house in the lane was Washingly Farm House belonging to Mr.&. Mrs. Juggins, they had two grown up children. Who were Monica and Roger, always referred to as Miss Monica and Master Roger by Mrs. Juggins

Mr. Juggins and Mr. Thackray were both 'Gentlemen' never meeting anyone without a word or two, even if they were in conversation with someone else at the time, and always raising their hats to the ladies with a cheery hello.

The next houses were known as 'the houses across the field' as they went with Washingly Farm and there was no made up road to them, access to them was through a farm gate and across the field. These houses were occupied by the people who worked for Mr. Juggins.

In the first one were Mr.&. Mrs. Harry Sewell and their family, all older than me. I only had contact at this time with the two younger boys. They were Douglas and Brian, nick named 'Nugget' and 'Flint,' I don't know the origins of these names. Mr. Sewell was a Shepherd to Mr. Juggins. Mr. Sewell had a Brother Sam who worked for Harry Raby at Brookfield Farm. (Mr. Sewell told me that his family moved to Great Stukeley from Devon.when they were young men.) Next to them was Mr.&. Mrs. Haynes with their two daughters and two sons, the girls were the elder ones, and I didn't have much contact with them. The two boys were Peter, who was older than me and Harry a little younger.

In the other house were Mr. &. Mrs. Ted Cox and their three daughters, Alice, who was about my age, and Lily and Angela who were younger. Mr. Cox was the horse keeper. He had a brother that lived in Godmanchester, and used to visit Ted some Sunday mornings. He was a slightly built man, no more than about nine stones, he was very sprawl footed, and walked at (ten to two), and rode his cycle on his heels. He had a nick name, which was, Slider, I am not sure how this came about. Possibly because the way he walked.

There was another family in the house that Mr. Haynes lived in for a short period of my memories, He was Mr. 'Ozzie' Hobbs, who was the eldest son of the fore mentioned Mr.&. Mrs. Hobbs. But I didn't really know much about him as he moved away, I think to Coventry, when I was about six years old.

The next house was Grange Farm, down a long 'Private' road, not maintained by the Council. 'The Grange' was farmed by Mr. George Gifford, as by this time his father Mr. Josh Gifford had passed on, although I do remember Mrs. Gifford just!. Mr. George Gifford was a fairly large man slightly bent forward, he had a ruddy complexion like all men that had an outdoor life. He had very large black bushy eyebrows and spoke with a gruff sort of tone. Mr. Gifford was not a married man, and was cared for by his housekeeper, Miss Cooper, a cousin of the Giffords. There is a family tie between these two names, as on some of the old grave stones in Gt. Stukeley Church yard, the surnames are Cooper-Gifford.

On my bike in Green End, showing Mr Juggins' Washingly Farm in the background

On my bike in my 'smart suit' showing the old railway carriage in the background, which had been made into a bungalow

After leaving Green End and turning along Ermine Street. Almost immediately on the left is a small track leading to two cottages, known as Vinegar Hill, at this time in the first one lived an elderly couple named Moon, Mr. Moon rode a tricycle. During the war he made wooden toys, which were sold in 'Claytons' a shop in Huntingdon. Toys at that time were very few and far between. I remember he used to smoke a pipe with a silver top that used to fold down over the bowl, maybe this was for when it rained? And in the other house lived Mr. & Mrs. Prior and their daughter Vivien, who was a little older than me.

Going on a little further, between the hills, was the Lodge Gate House leading to the front entrance to Great Stukeley Hall, which I will mention later. Mrs. Ruben Deller lived here with her five daughters, Mr. Deller had passed on before my time, all the girls were quite a bit older than me, Kathleen was the youngest, and then Ruby, both still at school when I started. All the others were grown up by this time, but I don't remember if they were all married at this time, but I knew them as Mrs. Rose Swan, Mrs. Betty Howes and Mrs. Alice Lyons.

Opposite Mrs. Deller was a farm roadway leading to Waterloo Farm owned by Mr. Fred Gifford, brother of George who also had similar bushy eyebrows. This farm is nearer to Brampton than Great Stukeley, and backs onto the race course. There were no houses on this road until it reached the farm. Here were two brick built cottages, and the much older farm house, about seventeenth century. One thing of interest along the road was a wind driven pump that supplied water to cattle troughs in the neighbouring fields. The pump was surrounded by a high metal fence for safety.

Mr. Fred married late in life, and didn't have any children, apparently Mr. Fred and his wife wanted to adopt me when I was a baby, saying to my Mother and Father, 'Let us have your little boy you are both young and can have more children, unlike us.' I understand this to be true as my parents often recalled the story.

Mr. Fred and his wife were very likeable people, not that I saw very much of them, mostly when my father was on loan to Mr. Fred by his brother George, as it was usually at week ends and I used to go with him. There was always a glass of lemonade and a home made cake for me, and lots of affection whenever I was there.

Next, on the left had side of Ermine Street were four council houses, these were the old type of the 1919 pattern. In the first one, Mr. Bert De'ath, always pronounced 'Death,' there were three daughters, all grown up and married at this time. They were Mrs. Curtis, (Tilly) Mrs. Brooker (Flossie) and Mrs. Blunt. (Vimy). Her name had something with the battle of 'Vimy Ridge' in the first world war. I have been told that Bert heard of her birth when he was in the trenches.

In the next house Mr.&. Mrs. Humphrey with two sons, about my parents age, Frank and Albert. Next were Mr.&. Mrs. Tom Walsh and their two sons, Peter the younger, about six years older than me, and Maurice, he was in the R.A.F in the war.

In the last one lived 'Granny' Waldock. Whose maiden name was, (yes here it is again) Deller. Her son Wally lived with her, with his wife and, at that time, a son Brian and daughter Sylvia, she being the elder, later there was another son, Trevor quite a bit younger than me.

Opposite these houses is Owl End.

Carrying on the main road, just after the Waldocks is a house called Denmark House at that time the people living there were named Grice but I didn't know much about them.

A little further along was a house with a large garden and some out buildings. Mr. Reg. Cade lived here with his wife Olive (Charlie Deller's Sister) and son Raymond. The house was called Sunnyside, Mr. Cade was a bus driver. The previous occupiers of this house were named Papworth, I don't remember them being there but I knew their son 'Jackie' later on as he married Ruby Deller. The last house along here before turning into Church Road was the Three Horse Shoes public house. A little more about this later on.

Now to Owl End. I will not dwell on this too much as this is where Mrs. Faulkner lived as a girl, and being an accomplished writer her book covers this road thoroughly. I will though, just mention the people and their houses as I remember them.

First there was the old village hall, (or W.I. Hall) a wooden building with a corrugated iron roof. This was used for various functions, for example Dances, Whist Drives, Wedding Receptions Concert Parties. I think it was also used for meetings, such as Cricket and Football Club, Parish Council and possibly others. I know it was used by the Home Guard for lectures and training films.

On the left side of the road there is the old College Farm where Mr. & Mrs. Ted Porter lived, as did Mr. Porter's Mother and Father, who was a retired London Policeman.

Next was another old house, Manor Farm where a Professor Parker Smith with his wife and a son Robin lived. In their garden was a small bungalow, Mrs. Parker Smith's Mother lived here, Mrs. Dudley-Mason and her daughter Miriam. Next also on the left was Mr.& Mrs. Cole and family. He was the head gardener at the hall. Next on the right is the rear entrance to the Hall. And a cottage occupied by people named 'Dick' Hudson and his wife. This was previously occupied by a family called Blair or Belairs, I can remember visiting them with my parents when I was very young, about six, the husband used to play the piano accordion, which was of interest to my parents, as my mother played the piano. Mostly hymns on Sundays, not that she was very religious, but apart from a song about Amy Johnson the famous aviator and an early wartime song, On A Wing and A Prayer were the only pieces of sheet music she had, all the other pieces were religious, passed on from her mother. My father used to play the piano by ear and was quite good on the mouth organ.

There were two other houses inside the hall grounds but I can't remember who lived there at the time.

Next on the right hand side lived Mr.&. Mrs. Wendholt and their three daughters, the elder being Margaret, (Now Mrs. Faulkner) and the twins, Marion and Irene. I remember Mrs. Wendholt being a great 'Blood Donor.' Further along on the right were two more houses, in the first one was Mr.&. Mrs. Brooker and their son David, Mr. Brooker was a bus driver. In the second house lived Mr. Allen I can't remember Mrs. Allen but they had two daughters, Nellie and Betty who I didn't know very well, Mr. Allen drove the Local Delivery railway lorry, I remember this being a three wheel Scamel articulated model. He always wore calf length black leather gaiters and a green baize apron.

Next on the left was a farm belonging to Mr. Baker, with a house and farm buildings. Which is Cartwright's Farm Next on the right were two more cottages, one was occupied by Mr.&. Mrs. 'Jup' Lyons they had a son, younger than me. In the other one at that time Mr.&. Mrs. Jack (yes here it is again) Deller. Further up the road was the last cottage, this was thatched and Mr.&. Mrs. Cobley Bill & Liz lived there.

Owl End then runs on to be a farm track, past Prestly Wood and over the railway bridge to Lodge Farm where I was born.

Before turning into Church End I will mention the Three Horse Shoes. The landlord at this time was Mr. Arthur Crow who lived there with his wife and son Arthur, always known as Young Arthur Crow.

With the pub were some nice out buildings and a small cattle yard also a small field, I don't think the field actually belonged to the brewery but it always went with the pub. Mr. Crow had two cows that he milked and brought milk round the village with the milk pails on the handlebars of his bicycle, these were oval shaped with tight fitting lids with brass bands and plaques on the lids, no doubt signifying that they were official milk carrying vessels. His customers would have to go out to him with their jugs and he would fill them with his correctly measured ladles these had long handles and hung on the side of the pails, these also had official looking plaques on.

Young Arthur Crow had a small farm in the parish of Woolley, it was situated where Huntingdon Life Sciences is now.

Now to Church End, as it was called then. Now Church Lane

On the right was a large farm house, with a small cottage attached. This is now the Three Horseshoes Restaurant. At the time of which I recall it was owned by farmers called, Golodetz. There were two brothers, I am not sure of their nationality but I think they were Polish. They lived in Little Stukeley but their land ran through both villages. In the main house lived Mr.&. Mrs. Gillett and their son Raymond, Mr. Gillett was a farm bailiff, I suppose he would now be called Farm Manager. In the cottage lived Mr. Ernest Cobley, whose son was lost in the war, at Dunkirk I think. A little further down on the left was Kitchener Terrace, this was a row of four cottages occupied at this time by Mr.&. Mrs. Ted Curtis and their daughter Gill, about my age, Mr. Curtis was a nursery man and worked for Wood & Ingram who owned what is now Frosts Garden Centre in Brampton. This was a much larger firm then, owning what is now the golf course and river lane, also land and buildings along Thrapston Road which is now Mr. 'Gren' Sewell's farm, also a large site in St. Germain Street in Huntingdon., now Sainsbury's car park, with an extensive greenhouse layout and a large warehouse, they also had a retail shop in George Street in Huntingdon where most local people would buy all their seed requirements and if necessary advice on all gardening aspects. I can well remember going there with my father. There was a large set of little square drawers, almost covering a whole wall with labels on signifying seeds inside, these were all loose and had to be weighed. All the seeds purchased were put into brown envelopes, but without the variety or name on. This was added at the time of purchase. A great number of Great Stukeley people would have know of this large company. Next was Mr.&. Mrs. Ernie Burton with their sons Lawrence and Derek, Lawrence is the elder, but younger than me. Mr. Burton was a Civil Engineer, I think he worked for a ministerial department, I know he held a position of foreman on the construction of the complex at Earith Sluice. Next were Mr.&. Mrs. Walter Gough and their sons John and George, John was the eldest, he worked for Chivers in Huntingdon. George is a little younger than me.

This is the Horsehoes Restaurant at the top of Church Road. When I was a boy it was the Farm House and Cottage

John joined the Royal Navy when he was old enough as did George later on. Mr. Gough worked at Grange Farm. He served in the army in the 1914/1918 war and was quite a bit older than my father, at some time he had lost an eye, not in the war. I think he had a mishap whilst chopping wood. He was the first person that I knew with a glass eye. The last one changed occupiers several times, I can't remember in what order, but 'Granny' Sly at one time and Miss Warne, who was a Music teacher. And one or two others

Next on the right were three detached bungalows in the first one Mr.&. Mrs. Rawlingson and their daughter Dorothea (DoDo) in the middle the Rev. Lewis Woolford our vicar lived. In the third one was Mr. and Mrs. Stratton. A little further down, still on the right was the old vicarage, then the church. (I will elaborate on these two places later) Next to the church was the old post office, run by Mrs. 'Granny' Bull. This is a thatched house, called Glebe Cottage, with the thatch coming almost to the ground at the church yard side. It is possibly the oldest house in the village now. I don't remember much about 'Granny' Bull, she seemed to me to be quite old when I first knew her, I remember her as being quite rounded, and deaf and sometimes a bit grumpy. I can't recall Mr. Bull I think he was lost in the First World War. Mrs. Bull had three children, all my parents generation. There were two daughters, and a son. The girls were Eva who married Bob Stukins who came from Offord, and was a postman. The other girl was Mary (also known as Meg) Was married to Denny Sly a sports photographer. The two ladies were well known in the village, because they always ready to join in and help with what ever activity was going on, and had lived in the village all of their lives. Mrs Bull's son Mr. Tom Bull, became Post Master at Huntingdon Post Office. It seemed that the whole family was connected to the postal service in some way or other. At one time this was a small farm, with buildings in the yard, and land running down parallel to the road and behind Moorfield cottages. In the same area was the sweet shop owned by Mrs. Allsop, I can remember going in the shop when I was at school from a very early age, about five I think, clutching my few coppers, and deciding what to buy. I can still remember the 'Gob Stoppers' bought for about a half penny at that time, I, like many others use to keep taking it out of my mouth to see if it had changed colour. There was also liquorice boot laces and other goodies. Next still on the right was a house owned by a Mr. Bill Johnson and his wife Lilly, who was Mrs. Alsop's daughter. Bill served in the R.A.F. during the war, and was away most of the time,we didn't see much of him. Bill had a niece called Marion Tasker, and she stayed with Lilly for most of the war.

We have now reached the end of Church Lane as a road, it was then a dead end, at the end was the school house where Miss Leppard the head teacher lived she had a large cat, it was her constant companion. To the left of this was the school playground, which sloped up to the main school. This was a traditional Victorian school building At the bottom of this was a wooden slatted fence, and a hedge of lavender In the same site was the infant's school, where one would be taught up to the age of seven, before moving up to the 'Big' School. I think the infant's school had been a chapel of some sort. Between the infant's school and Rose Cottage was a narrow path leading up to a cottage occupied by a Mr.&. Mrs. Maile and their daughter Jean. Jean was head girl at the school, and I can remember her standing in as temporary teacher for us in the infants department if the other teacher was away for any reason. Mr. Maile was a builder and worked for a firm in Huntingdon, Stanley Brawn (Builders)

This is the Old School House, at the end of what is known as Church End, where Miss Leppard lived until she retired

This is where Church End came to a stop with a five bared gate and a hand gate we used to call 'Kissing Gate'. This opened up to green fields, Moorfield, until 1948. The white house in the background is one of twelve built at the time

Next also on the left of the school house is a house called Rose Cottage, where Mr.& Mrs. Steve Eaton lived, they had a large black barn on the opposite side of the path which backed onto the school house, in this he kept a few cows, the barn had a rear door which opened onto a grass field, (Moor Field) which is no longer there. Mr. and Mrs. Eaton had a French lady living with them, I didn't really know her, but she was always called Mademoiselle From this point there was a tarmac path this carried on up a slight slope, just here was another old house, where 'Granny' Papworth lived, no relation to 'Jackie's' family. This house has also disappeared under the new development. She had two sons of my parent's generation, I think they both served in the army during the war, they were Dick and Arthur, Dick had a son Richard the same age as me, but they lived in Huntingdon. A little further up the path on the right hand side was a small wooden bungalow, where Miss. Leppard retired to, opposite this were some allotments. A short distance after this the path turned sharp left, through the kissing gate where Moor field Way started, from here it was the cinder path, at this time the old council house gardens came right down to this point. The path continued on and emerged onto Ermine Street, opposite Owl End.

To the right of the school house was a five barred gate and a hand gate leading onto the grass field, this field was called Moor Field and the houses called Moor Field Cottages, with a farm track leading onto other fields. Here were two cottages on the right.

At this time Mr. & Mrs. Gilbert lived in the right hand one with their two sons, Dennis and Bernard, Dennis was the younger one, but both older than me.. Next door was Mr. &. Mrs. Gough, yes I have mentioned them before and will again before my story ends. Slightly round a corner some fifty yards or so were two more cottages, one was occupied by,(yes here we are again) Mr.&. Mrs. David Deller, and their son also David, I think there was a daughter, I can't quite remember, but they would have been my parents age. At the time Mr.&. Mrs. Joe Turton lived in the other one with their three children, Dorothy, Raymon,(yes this is the correct spelling) and Iris, Dorothy being much the elder, next came Raymon, a little older than me and then Iris the youngest, a little younger than me. I believe Mr. Turton moved down to this area during the big depression, 1926/ 1930s. His family moved down from Sheffield seeking a better life. Mr. Turton, having been a miner, had to turn his hand to other work. Unfortunately, unlike the rest of the family, Joe was not the most pleasant of men. Being unwell most of the time probably had something to do with this. Other members of the family, Mrs. Turton's brother his wife and children also came down at the same time. Their name was Brentwood. Mr. Brentwood was a plumber, and he worked for F.B. Thakary in Huntingdon. They all spoke with a broad Yorkshire accent, a little difficult to grasp at times. I had the pleasure of getting to know Mr. Brentwood well, as when I left school I became an apprentice plumber.

Mrs. Turton also had a sister living near by, I am not sure where exactly. I don't remember her married name, I didn't know much about her when I was a boy.

I am sure she was in the nursing profession, as a young man I remember as being matron at Shortsands nursing home in St. Neots.

That just about tidies up Church Lane as it was then. A lot more houses now!

Early Days

My earliest memories are from about the age of four. I remember Doug and Brian Sewell taking me to school, they were about eleven and twelve at that time. Apparently they asked my mother if I could go to school as they would look after me, after clearing it with Miss Leppard. According to my mother they didn't always look after me that well, but we all know what mothers are like with their little boys. Sometimes they would hold my hands and make me run with them, other times they would run on ahead and leave me, then hide behind a tree, as we use to go across the field at the back of our house then across The Park which had lots of nice big trees, I think all in all they were good to me. I had a little peddle car at one time, I think my parents must have bought it second hand, as I am sure they wouldn't have been able to afford a new one, as farm workers wages were very low at that time. Doug and Brian use to push me up and down the road sometimes, and one day they pushed me into Mr. Deller's hedge and Mother happened to see this and she as out in a flash, they got a good telling off for that.

At that time Mrs. Cobley lived in the cottage 'Round the Corner' and I used to knock on her back door saying, 'Cobbles let me in' as that was what I called her. I remember she was a kindly lady, older than my parents. She had two grown up daughters. She moved away to Oundle, I think she had family there. She wasn't related to the other Coblys in the village. My Mother and I went to see her once, I don't know how we got there, it may have been by bus via Thrapston, which was quite a journey for my mother, as she wasn't used to travelling.

At that age I don't think we did much at school, I remember we had sand trays to draw in and slate boards and chalk. We use to cut out pictures from old magazines with blunt round- nosed scissors, and fraying, that was pulling apart small squares of material into single strands. The girls used this to stuff little pillows for their dolls beds. There were other activities like learning to read and write, but I have no real memory of such uninteresting things!

Sometimes we would play hunt the thimble. I remember once looking for Easter Eggs. It may have been only one year, as after 1939 sweets were on ration. I think Miss Fisher was still teaching the infants when I first went to school, she was the daughter of the landlord of The Three Horseshoes. They kept the pub prior to Mr. Crow. Miss Smith was the infants teacher then until the school closed. Miss Smith lived in Huntingdon and cycled to Great Stukeley School, I remember her as having a roundish face and a bright red complexion.

Our next door neighbour was Mr. Bates who was known as 'Ratty Bates' and it fitted him well. He was quite an old man and had a daughter my mother's age. I remember one day playing ball by myself and it went on his garden. He was there so I asked if I could have my ball back. It was a soft rubber one. He looked at me and then at my ball and instead of getting it for me, he chopped it with his hoe. 'Ratty' Indeed!

When I was about six, I was going to school on my own; I think Doug and Brian had left by then. My mother had a little job in Huntingdon cleaning for an old couple on Mondays. On these days I used to take an egg to Mrs. Rubin Deller, which was my way to school, and she would cook it for my dinner, I would go to her house with her daughter Kathleen and then back to school. No school meals then of course, we all went home for lunch.

Great Stukeley School was a Church of England school, so had close ties with the Church. I remember the vicar used to come to the school on alternate Friday mornings, on the other Fridays we had to go up to the church. We also had to attend Sunday school. In the summer time, on some Sundays, the vicar would have us for tea on the lawn, where we had bread and jam and cups of tea. We were segregated, boys one week and girls the next. The vicar had a parrot called Arthur, who would climb up a tree and squawk and sometimes refuse to come down.

Great Stukeley Church was regarded as 'High Church.' I think it was referred to as being Anglo Catholic; I remember the incense in the smoking container being swung to and fro while the Vicar was walking up the aisle and people taking Holy Communion.

When the Rev Bagley of All Saints in Huntingdon took over from The Rev. Lewis Woolford some of the more deeply religious services were changed. For instance I can't remember the incense being used after that.

I can't remember the year, probably when rationing started, when we all had to assemble in the main school for our weekly dose of Cod Liver Oil & Malt, we would line up in front of the stove, which was a large round cast iron heater with a guard round it, and someone would come along with the big jar and a spoon, and we had to 'open wide' and would be fed with the 'mixture,' I am sure we all shared the same spoon! I can't remember all the lessons we had but I can recall Miss Leppard reading to us on Friday afternoons. The most remembered story was Children of the New Forest. Most of us were quite attentive as she made it very interesting by explaining things as she went along, not just reading the pages. This was a very large book. Sometimes she would try to teach us music. For this there was a large rolled glossy looking canvas with the notes set out like sheet music. The lines, symbols and notes were all of different colours to make it easier for us to understand, hopefully!

She was a well built lady with greying hair and glasses. She had slightly protruding front teeth. On special days like May Day for instance she would come to school dressed in her cap and gown. I remember the 'May Pole' coming out on mayday, which was held on Ascension Day, as it was a Church school. The girls used to do the dancing, making several different patterns round the pole, and an arrangement like a tent. We boys were much too butch for any dancing, but sometimes we had to stand on the base to stop the pole falling over. Also we had to take turns at recitations or singing. I remember once I had to recite a poem about a Cock Sparrow, just right for me as I had a nice little brown/fawn suit ideal for a sparrow.

There was A May Queen, as was the tradition, and one year the Queen was my sweetheart Margaret Wendholt, lovely girl then and always has been.

I wonder if Miss Leppard realized that the May pole was a pagan fertility symbol? Maybe not, she was a very religious person I don't think that sort of thing would ever have entered her head!

The War Years

When the London Blitz started, we like many other families had an evacuee billeted with us, a nice little girl. She was the same age as me and her mother came as well. They were Mrs. Perry and her daughter Pauline, but they only stayed about six months. My parents told me later, when they thought I would understand, that the Perry family agreed that if they were going to be bombed 'that they would all go together.' Soon after Pauline went home, we were allocated another evacuee this time a boy. His name was George Stillwell. When he first came he was very timid and afraid, because he had been treated very badly by his previous 'carers' but my parents soon got him settled, and he stayed with us until the war ended. He was, and still is like the brother I never had, my parents always referred to him as 'our other boy'

Mrs. Owen had a boy living with her during the war and a little after, Brian Smith. He was not a true evacuee, I think he was distantly related to either Mr. or Mrs. Owen. He actually lived in St Ives his father was in the army, he used to visit when he was on leave. I don't remember his mother being mentioned, maybe he didn't have one.

When I was ten years old the education system changed, and at the age of eleven we had to attend a larger school. As I was already getting towards eleven it was arranged that I should change schools at that time, as one member of the family, George, was being moved it seemed right that we should go together, although I did have to go to the junior department for about one term.

I am sure that it was also an advantage for the pupils left in the village schools. Until then teachers had to cope with seven to fourteen year olds all in the same class room. A bit of a hand full no doubt for any teacher.

Mother and Father with Mrs Perry, Pauline and me

Pauline with me on my bike

*Mother and Father (in his Home Guard uniform)
with George and I*

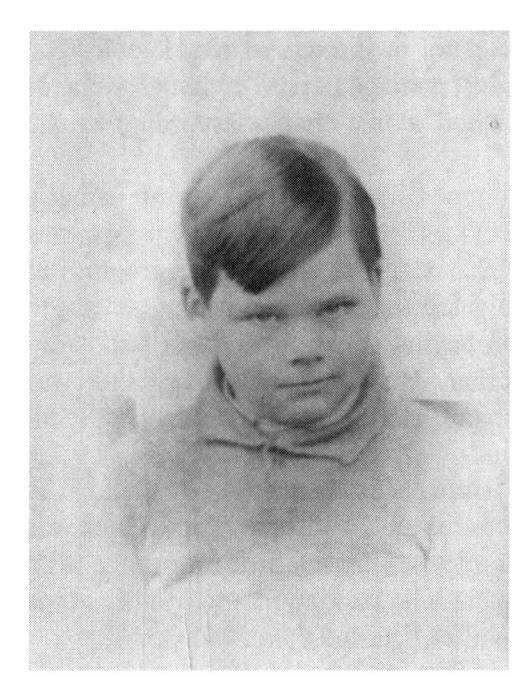

Left: *School photo of me with my 'Coy' look*

Below left: *Another picture showing my first fountain pen bought for me by George's parents we both had the same type of pen. They were 'Mentmore' pens, collectable now*

Below right: *Another school picture, this time showing my 'Bunny Badge'*

Having started Huntingdon School at the age of ten, I took 'The Eleven Plus' exam there. I didn't manage to pass, although some of my teachers thought that I stood a fair chance according to the school tests.

I was told later on that I probably failed because of Father's occupation, 'Farm Worker'. That maybe, but I have no regrets about not passing I don't think I suffered any lack of progress in life because of it. I have always felt that at school you are taught to learn, and that your education begins after school. Four pupils did pass. They were Thelma Horner. Janet Spicer, whose father was the manager of the bus company, Bob Tanner and Mr. Davis, all from 'The North End' of town.

The school that became Brook Side was always called, 'The Council School.' When I started there Mr. Harry (Pop) Slater was the head master, Mr. John Stapleton was senior form master Miss (Polly) Burr was a senior teacher who had taught my Mother at the same school. She retired soon after I started there.

There were no School buses then, so we all had to cycle or walk to school. George and I had cycles. There were no school meals then, so we had to take sandwiches, or eat in the town. George and I mostly had sandwiches. We did try the 'British Restaurant' which was situated in the basement of one of the buildings attached to, and belonging to Trinity Church. The meals were not all that good, I don't think they would have been expensive. There was sometimes a bit of friction with children from another school. On one occasion we almost got into a fight in the restaurant and were warned that if we didn't behave, we would be banned. We had good reason to threaten a fight, at least we thought so, some of the boys from the other school had taken Harry Haynes's hat and were throwing it around. Eventually it went over a wall. That is when we thought that was enough and started a bit of a ruck! This was a public restaurant not just for school children, so I suppose some sort of order was necessary, so as not to upset the other customers.

When I was thirteen the education system changed again, for some students there was an opportunity to try for the Grammar school again. All pupils over the age of eleven had to leave both

Godmanchester and the Common school, and attend Brook side Secondary. The classes were then much larger, and that is when Streaming was installed.

This was a system where each years class was divided and designated into A. B. or C stream, to accommodate pupils of varying abilities

Soon after this there was another change to the education system. School leaving age went up from fourteen to fifteen. A few of us were caught up in the change, having already having had a full year in the top class, we had to stay for a further year. This meant sitting in with the pupils just being promoted to that class, and going through the same lessons again.

I was friendly with a boy called Geoffrey Maile. We sat together on double desks; I was on the inside next to the wall, and Jeff next to the aisle.

We used to have student teachers take lessons as part of the teacher training. One such student was Mr. Tom Peck, a local boy his parents lived in St. Peters road. One day when he was patrolling up and down the class room, as they did, Jeff was messing about doing something, and didn't see Mr. Peck coming up from behind, and when he drew level he took a swipe at Jeff with the book he was carrying, Jeff ducked and it hit me, I jumped up and was going to hit him, but being close to the wall I couldn't get at him, so I told him I would fight him.

Weighing over ten stones, I think I may have frightened him. He was no bigger than me. We resented having to call him Mr. He wasn't much older than us.

When the Senior Master, John Stapleton arrived to sort things out he said if there was going to be any fighting it would be with him. I didn't fancy that at all, he was a big man over six feet tall, and an ex university rugby man.

There was another time that I was at odds with a member of staff, the music teacher, Miss Bradshaw. she asked the question. ' Who has a musical instrument at home and what is it?' I put my hand up. 'And what have you got?' I replied that my mother has a piano. 'What sort of piano?' she asked. 'An upright iron grand' I answered.

'There is no such thing as an upright grand' said Miss Bradshaw, 'it is either an upright or a grand.' I argued that that is what it is, because it says 'Upright Iron Grand ' Made in London under the lid and can clearly be seen when it is being played. It has a cast iron frame like a grand but it stands upright, I used to take off the front lower panel and play it like a harp. 'Don't argue with me' she said, go and stand outside, 'and you Maile go with him,' because he was laughing.

When Mr. Slater the head came along and saw us standing in the corridor we explained the situation to him, and he said that I shouldn't argue with Miss. Bradshaw.

I don't think he wanted to cane us for this, so he gave us a lecture about respect and sent us to Mr. Stapleton for extra lessons as punishment.

Because we had to serve another year, the school wasn't geared up for us, and no preparations had been put into place for the extra year students, so the school didn't know what to do because there were only a few of us.

John Stapleton suggested that Jeff and I took extra maths and any other subject we fancied. We said that we weren't keen on the music class as we were taught only singing. Neither Jeff or I could sing so didn't like it.

That suited me as I liked maths. We also had extra history and geography. We were set different work from the other students, even though we sat in the same room.

Some of the maths were quite advanced for us, Mr. Stapleton started us on 'Logarithms' and geography that we hadn't covered before.

He really tried to make sure that our extra year wasn't wasted, and as long as we tried, he helped us all the way, while still taking a full class of thirteen to fourteen year olds.

That is what I call a dedicated teacher.

When Mr. Slater was in a bad mood he had a habit of passing from room to room, through the interconnecting doors stern faced and not speaking to anyone not even the teacher taking the class, with his cane sticking up the back on the inside of his jacket with his hands behind him holding the handle. The cane was rather thin, quite swishy. He was rather like fencer wanting to draw his sward, and woe betide any one that gave him cause to do so. I left school on the same day as Mr. Stapleton, I was helping him clear out his cupboard, when I came across his gym shoes, about size twelve, which he used for punishment. On picking them up he said 'you haven't had one of these have you,' 'no' I said, so he gave me a whack across the back side saying, 'Well you have now,' with a big grin on his face. He left the secondary school to take over the headship at Brampton School.

Very early in the war, the 'Home Guard' was formed, and my Father had to join. Farm workers were classified as reserved occupation. Some married men were exempt, but single men were liable to be called up. The men had to assemble at the village hall on Sunday mornings for training etc. Uniforms were issued, along with rifles (eventually)! But they had no ammunition. I can remember as part of their training, holes being dug large enough for a man to stand in, with covers over them. These would have been used to attack tanks, the idea was to dig these holes where tanks would run should we be invaded, and when the tanks were overhead the man would open his cover and plant a 'Sticky Bomb' to the underside of the tank. On the bank opposite the blacksmiths shop at the end of Green End, slit trenches were dug so that the road could be defended in case of attack. A little further down the road towards Huntingdon, a large barrel of waste oil was placed, ready to tip onto the road so as to make a Skid Pan for oncoming vehicles. The bank at this point was much wider then, as the road has been altered a few times. I remember that there was some controversy about the training, I think the officer in charge was an 'Honorary' position, and required no military training, and this was resented by some of the old soldiers, who had been drafted into the home guard, and had fighting experience in the first world war, so this situation didn't go down very well.

Education carried on, but out of school hours were much more exciting. George and I weren't allowed to play in our school clothes. We had to change into our 'play clothes' when we got home. Clothes were expensive, and on 'coupons,' part of the rationing process. Also due to rationing, boys were only allowed to wear short trousers, and men's were not allowed turn ups.

There were no playing or sports equipment at Great. Stukeley School, but my father would make most things that boys would want, like cricket bats and wickets toy guns for games like cowboys, and war games. We had hoops from old bicycle wheels and home made whipping tops We seemed to have all we wanted, either made or improvised with a bit of imagination. We were brought up to respect things, and people. Harsh discipline was not necessary, but sometimes we would get a bit of a slap from mother, if she could catch us! no doubt we deserved it. We weren't 'Angels.' Mischievous rather than malicious would describe us I think.

We spent a lot of time in or around the park, as this was only just across the grass field at the back of our house, I think we knew every tree, and had climbed most of them.

There was a spinney right along our side of the park separating it from Mr. Gifford's fields, which we knew equally well, as my father worked for him. We had what one might call, a roving commission, as long as we behaved ourselves. I recall one particular incident with Mr. Gifford. George and I were walking across a field of wheat, it was only about two inches high, when he came galloping along on his horse, saying, in not a very pleasant manner. 'If you must walk across my fields, walk up the rows not across them, you are flattening the crop,' oblivious to the damage he was doing, kicking up great divots of earth and corn with his galloping horse.

There is a small wooded area about a mile from where our old house used to be, called 'Prestley' wood, some people called it 'The Bluebell Wood.' It is not very big, about three or four acres at that time. A lot of it was lost at a later date when Alconbury Airfield was extended to take the larger planes, and to re-align the runways. In the wood is a moat, surrounding an island it was mostly dry, except in a very wet season. Historians tell that this is the site of the one time Prestley Manor House. I don't know if it has ever been excavated. Maybe we should send for 'The Time Team!' It was a very popular place for people to visit. My father used to take me there some times when he went pigeon shooting. There was an old fallen tree across the moat and he would carry me over this on his shoulders if there was water in it, then build a 'Hide' in which we would have to sit very quietly, (difficult for me), until the pigeons came in to roost.

Once whilst playing on a tree in the park, a branch cracked. Unfortunately for us Mr. Cole the gardener saw us, I don't think he liked children very much, even though he had some of his own. They were girls, maybe it was just boys he disliked. On this occasion before we could get home he was at our house giving my mother a bit of a hard time verbally. I don't think any boys in the village liked him as most of us had crossed swords with him at some time or other. He was always known as 'Old Coley.' Another time he caught us playing on the swings and roundabout in the hall grounds, these were of a very good quality, made by the Wicksteed Co, as in Wicksteed Park. Unseen by us Mr. & Mrs. Cole came through the garden shouting at us, but we were too quick for them, and jumped over the railings we could hear Mrs. Cole shouting repeatedly to her husband ' Call the police.' But nothing ever came of this encounter.

There was a nice orchard in the corner of the park, quite close to the Hall. We would sometimes nip in to 'scrump' an apple or two, but never more than we could eat there and then.

Our old house was part of a much larger one, probably altered about two hundred years or so earlier. I think the original house was seventeenth century, or maybe earlier and would have been thatched, as were the two houses opposite. I believe this is so because the roof was tiled, and the roof line at the back was much lower and covered the extension which was single story. There was no break in the roof angle or line, and all the tiles were the same, indicating that they were all laid at the same time during the alterations. The extension was built in brick and formed a scullery carrying on along to the next house in the same manner. I think that the cottage round the corner may have been built at the same time, along with a communal wash house with a copper built in the corner. The ladies would choose which day would be their wash day, the copper would be filled the night before by the men, and the wood for the fire brought in ready for morning. This was also our bath house. It may have been living in fairly primitive times, but we were clean! There was also a three unit soil closet, one for each dwelling, with the usual wooden box that had a hole in the top and the closet pail underneath, which had to be emptied regularly. There was no night soil cart at this time, so householders made their own arrangements. There was no toilet paper so news paper was used, sometimes one was lucky enough to get the tissue paper off oranges at Christmas, when they were available. News paper was O.K. but it was unfortunate if one was reading something, then couldn't find the next square to continue.

Another of the alterations was to the chimney in the living room where the old black range was. Obviously this at one time had been an 'Ingle Nook' type of fireplace. When the work was carried out, a new brick chimney was built inside the original opening, but only up to about three feet above the ground floor ceiling.

The original beam that went across the inglenook was still in place and had not been covered over, when you looked behind it you could see where it use to get scorched.

When Mother had the sweep in, he could only sweep the lower part of the chimney, as the new chimney only went up a short distance. When the sweep had swept the lower part he had to go upstairs, through the first bedroom, as this opened directly at the top of the stairs, and one had to pass through this to get to the other two. In the far bedroom there was a cupboard with a door that opened up into the original large chimney, this was about eight feet by six feet, tapering off to about one and a half feet square, Where the new chimney entered the original, it left a large ledge all the way round where the soot collected, which had to be swept off. This ledge area was so large you could have hidden at least ten men there.

Our old house at Green End

My father told me that when the old place was demolished, they had to use two tractors to pull the beams apart, this was in 1961. My parents were allocated a council bungalow in 1960. No chance of houses being that strong now. Once when some repairs were being carried out and the front wall was exposed, the old 'Mud and Stud' plaster was revealed. This was a method of building in that period, (seventeenth century) the stud work was of rough sawn or split timbers in the uprights, and split hazel woven in between. The plaster was locally dug mud mixed with straw and spread by hand, squeezing the mixture into the hazel laths. The mud would have been dug near the building, providing that it was clay soil. That is why there is almost always a pond near these old buildings, where the mud was dug from.

Mother and father about 1939/40 at back of the old house

We had no electricity or water supply to any of the houses until just after the war. The water came first, but we didn't have electricity until about 1950. Even when the water supply was installed there was only one tap between the four dwellings, that was just inside our neighbour's garden, so we all had to carry our water from there into the house. Up until this time we drank water from a well, I don't think it did us any harm, because we all seemed to be healthy enough. All the village was in the same situation. There was a saying that if there were newts in the well, then the water was O.K. because they only stayed in good water.

For lighting we had a double wick oil lamp for the main room, which would stand in the middle of the table. How people managed I don't know. Mother, like all other women at that time, used to do all her knitting and sewing in that light, but it didn't seem to affect her sight as she didn't need glasses until she was well into her seventies.

For all other lighting we had candles. That was alright unless it blew out half way up the stairs. One would have to shield the flame with ones hand when moving from one room to another to prevent this. Candles were great for making shadows on the wall. It was surprising how many shapes you could make. I remember my Father showing us how to make faces and birds, also different dogs faces. Early home entertainment!.

I was fairly good at figures at an early age. There were always cards and dominoes being played at home, which was a good way to learn adding and subtracting. We had a lodger in about 1940 he was Bill Spinks, and a cribbage fanatic. He worked on Alconbury Aerodrome when it was an R.A.F. Station.

Sometimes Bill would have the crib board and cards out before Mother could get the table cleared from the evening meal. For those who do not play cribbage, one way of scoring is to make cards add up to 15, with 2,3, or 4 cards, I think I knew every combination of how to make 15 by the time I was six. Likewise with dominoes, adding the numbers at each end of the run then dividing by 5 or 3, hence the game of fives and threes. We also had a dart board and friends would come in for a game, when I was a little older I could add and subtract the scores quite well.

Once when the men were playing darts, one hit a wire, and it came back off the board and stuck in the top of my head, I was about six at the time, and I have been told that I ran round the table several times crying out that I had a dart in my head. Some of my family have said that, 'I have never been right in the head since.'

Although things were scarce due to rationing, Mother always seemed to be able to rustle up something for birthday parties for us. We used to be invited to other parties, and friends were invited to ours. Mother would somehow manage to assemble the ingredients for a birthday cake, and often 'Granny' Papworth would make it for her, not that Mother couldn't, but Mrs. Papworth was a well known cake maker.

We had the usual games, like pass the parcel, blind mans buff, and especially the kissing game Postmans Knock, if you don't know of this game, you don't know what you have missed. Especially if your childhood sweetheart is there!

George and I weren't always on our own, far from it, we would often meet up with the other boys for rambles through the village, exploring all sorts of nooks and crannies, often being eyed up and down by adults, to see if we were getting into mischief, as if we would! Also playing games that needed more than two people. One of our favorite places was a spot called 'Cozen Hole.' This was just towards Little Stukeley down the hill from The Three Horseshoes. This was a wide ditch, mostly dry, and the bushes were very high and met over the top, ideal for adventure games. This ditch ran under the main road in a large culvert which we would get into and hear the traffic going over the top. Quite often a tramp, would spend the night under the bushes. We would see these men quite often, either with an old pram, or a large bundle with all their belongings in. Some times they would come up into the village. Not begging, mostly asking politely for some hot water to make their tea with, but hoping for a little more. My mother never refused them and often gave then something to eat. 'There is a poor man down on his luck' she would say.

We sometimes had a visit from constabulary! This was in the form of a very large policeman, or so he seemed to us. He used to ride round the village occasionally, coming up from Huntingdon on his bicycle. This was a big old thing with 28' wheels and a double crossbar. If he saw two or three boys together, he would call out to us. 'Now you boys, stand still.' He would get off his bike and take off his bicycle clips, place them in his top pocket, then take off his gauntlets, he held these in one hand and slap them into his other palm whilst talking to us, the conversation would be something like.

'What are you boys up to then?'

'Nothing.'

'You can't be doing nothing, where are you going?'

'Nowhere.'

'You can't be doing nothing or going nowhere, so, what are you really doing?'

We eventually told him because if we had given him any cheek, I am sure we would have had a slap with those ominous looking gauntlets. We never did give him any lip, and I am sure he never expected any. Then he would go through the procedure of replacing his cycle clips and gauntlets, give us a big grin and say. 'Off you go then boys.'

Of cause most boys had a catapult then. If we heard of a load of gravel or stones being delivered news would have been round the village in a shot, almost before the delivery lorry had gone. Then we would all swoop on it like vultures, looking for all the round stones, ammunition for our catapults. The code word was. 'ammo for catto!'

Although George was a London boy, he was fully at home with nature and village life. Bird nesting was popular during the nesting season George and I would go miles looking for nests all over the farm. We would find not only the common ones like blackbirds and thrushes. Thrushes were plentiful then, unlike to-day. We would find the nests of skylarks, plovers, yellow hammers, hedge sparrows, jackdaws in holes in trees. Magpies made thorny nests with roofs on. Nests of game birds like pheasants and partridge were out of bounds, although we would know where several of them were. We would sometimes find the odd wild duck nest in the ditches, sometimes they built their nests in a tree out of reach of stoats and foxes. When the ducklings were only one day old they had to jump down onto the ground, sometimes from a height of ten feet or more, where they ran to their mother, calling them from below. She took them to the nearest water, where they could find their own food; unfortunately they were still vulnerable to the predators. Robins' nests were mostly in garden hedges or sheds, they would often build in an old flower pot or something similar.

People would place old pots in their hedges to encourage the robins to nest. We didn't divulge our finds, as some boys would have had a collection which they would have liked to add to. Not us, we had too much respect for nature, although it was not illegal then.

Swallows use to build under the eaves on our old house. We would watch them working away with their little pieces of wetted mud until they had a complete rounded dome, with just enough room to get in and out. We could with some difficulty, lean right out of the bedroom windows and look into the nest. Often with a rebuke from mother, saying 'Leave the swallows alone, or they will forsake the nest!' One type of nest that was considered fair game were moorhens eggs, as they were good to eat. At that time Moorhens flourished in large numbers, sometimes as many as four nests on one pond. The way of getting these eggs was to take one of Mothers table spoons and tie it onto the end of her clothes prop, and try to reach the eggs from the bank, we often dropped them into the water, which was annoying. Moorhens usually laid about seven to ten eggs, so we would wait until there were about four or five in the nest, before they started to incubate, then take probably two from each nest. We found a much easier way of harvesting the eggs. Derek Burton had a one man rubber dinghy, (Survival Kit For A Pilot). George and I had a Stamp collection, nothing of any value I think. But we swapped it for Derek's dinghy. That made Moorhens nesting much easier. But it worried Mother when we went out in it.

Another sport was playing Conkers. We had a very large horse chestnut tree in the corner of the field at the back our house where it joined the spinney, which produced large numbers of the desired ammunition. We would collect all that we needed, make the required hole with father's awl or a nail through the middle and thread the string through, an old shoe lace seemed to be the best thing for this. Then when we were all ready we would go up into the main area of the village and all join in the battle to see who had the best conker, often going home with bruised knuckles and snagged fingers. 'Serves you right,' mother would say!

One of our other activates was to collect fire wood, for kindling. We would search the hedgerows and trees, looking for the old pieces of dead wood and break them up to go into a sack. Green wood didn't burn easily, and was of no use to start a fire. This kindling was mainly for the fire in the copper in the wash house, and the cooking range in the living room. This was the old type of stove with an oven on the side, and hot plates on the top which had removable rings, so as to be able to speed up the cooking, or quickly bring the saucepans up to boiling point. Mother had to clean this stove with black lead polish using brushes. And it used to shine beautifully. Coal was the best fuel for ranges. Wood would burn O.K. but controlling the temperature was difficult. Mother, like most country women, was a very good cook, learned at a very early age.

When she was only fourteen, she could bake cakes and pastries to perfection, and roast joints, all requiring different temperatures that were controlled with just one sliding damper in the flue, no thermostats then! We used to burn wood on the fire in the front room, but that was only on Sundays and days when we had visitors. This wood would be collected by my Father with a tractor and trailer around the farm, from fallen trees. If a large tree had to be felled on demand, to help the war effort, it would be carried out by the professionals from the saw mills, on the orders of some ministerial department or other. When this was done the men on the farm would be able to clear what was called, 'the top' which meant any small branches and brush wood not suitable for use in the mill. All the men on the farm had a share in this including the farm house, but mostly it was left to the men. It would be stored in a 'wood pile' at home, and eventually sawn up by my Father, with a little help from us boys, and placed in the wood shed to keep dry for burning in the winter. There is nothing like a nice wood fire to brighten up gloomy days. There is a saying that, you get two warms from a wood fire, one when you cut it up and one when you burn it.

George and I had an official job for a time in the war, we were the salvage collectors, which was organized by Miss. Monica Juggins. We had a red badge made of Bakelite, and called 'The Cog In The Wheel.' I learned later it was the symbol of the Lady Tablers, which was and still is the female branch of The Round Table.

My Father made us a sturdy four wheeled truck with steering, a bit like the soapbox but stronger. He painted it black and on the side, in white he wrote the words, 'The Star Salvage Company,' with a big white star. It was our pride and joy. We had to go round the houses and collect all the waste paper and aluminium, if there was any. There had been a national appeal for aluminium 'to build a Spitfire.' I learnt in later life that this was just a war time ruse to get people to save for the war effort. You couldn't build a Spitfire from old pots and pans! Our Green End store was in Mr. Thackray's barn. Salvage from other parts of the village was stored in one of the buildings at the old rectory in Church End. Our contribution would have been collected on a County system.

Another of our hobbies was to go onto the railway bridge at Lodge Farm, train spotting. We couldn't see the numbers or the names from above, but could from further down the line where the track was above ground level. The main point of the exercise was to count the trucks, and try to work out what they were carrying. The open ones were nearly always coal, going south. The longest train we counted was of empty coal trucks going back up north, we counted one hundred and ten trucks, and it seemed ages going by.

We used to try and drop small stones into these trucks as they passed under us, until one day my Father saw us, when he was working in a field close by. When he came home we got a stern warning, that if he saw us or heard that we had been doing it again, we would be restricted to home ground. That warning was enough, as it would have meant that our roving would have been ended for some time. All he required of us was respect, good manners and honesty. Even when we did something quite bad, as long as we owned up to it, which is all it took for him to be satisfied that we understood right from wrong.

With regard to respect, especially towards other people, I remember when I was about fourteen, after a visit up to the main village, I said to my Father

'Wally Waldock wants to see you sometime.'

'Who wants to see me?' he asked.

'Wally Waldock,' I replied.

'Who wants to see me?' he asked again.

'Mr. Waldock' I replied.

'Ah! That's better,' Father said, 'and what does Mr. Waldock want?'

'I think he wants you to sharpen a saw for him,' I replied.

There was always something of interest for us, so we didn't want for much. We were always able to make our own entertainment, even if there wasn't much going on in the village. We were always doing things our own way, making camps, climbing trees, collecting things, It is surprising for instance how many different shapes and colours one can find in a heap of stones, all that sort of thing was of interest to us. We liked going round the farm watching the men working either with horses or tractors. sometimes we would join in, unless we were told, 'Keep out of the way, boy,' then we would find something else to do, there was never a dull moment.

All along the road from Huntingdon were telegraph lines, these were mounted on double poles with several cross bars and insulation 'cups' made of porcelain to support the wires. I can't remember how many wires there were, even though we would have counted them at some time, there must have been at least 200, because they needed double poles for support. They would have made excellent targets for catapult practice, but we wouldn't dare, as someone would have seen us. There was a metal plaque on one of the posts opposite where Mr. Reg. Cade lived near The Three Horseshoes, giving warning that anyone causing damage to the installations would be prosecuted. We were told that this was put in place to warn Jackie Papworth, who lived there at the time.

These lines continued on to Little Stukeley, where they terminated into the large Telephone Exchange, this building has now been converted into a children's nursery, but it was there in the wartime, and for sometime after. There were also telephone lines running along side the railway track though not as many as along the road, I don't know if these were for G.P.O. or if they were for the railway company. This was The London & North Eastern Railway Company.

Our entertainment was generally held at the Village Hall.

There were whist drives, dances, meetings, and wedding receptions. There was also the village fete which was held in the park adjacent to the village hall, although sometimes at Great Stukeley Hall. The fete had the usual entertainments with Fancy Dress, Hoopla, Children's Races and Bowling For The Pig. Another game was to drop a penny coin onto a sixpenny piece in a bath of water, if you covered the sixpence there was a prize. Sometimes there were pony rides, the pony being loaned by Mr. Juggins.

One year at the garden fete my Father won the 'Bowling for a pig.' But on this occasion there was no pig, instead the prize was a small barrel of beer. It was four and a half gallons that was called a Small 36er. Being 36 pints. I remember my Father saying jokingly at the time, that the amount of people wanting a glass of Arthur's beer, that it should have been a Big 36er. That is 36 gallons.

My father had another piece of luck at about this time. There was a small pools company called 'The Dinkum' run from Peterborough, Mr. Ted. Curtis was the local agent. My Father had the good fortune to have a small win, a sum of eight pounds. At the time I think his basic wage was under four pounds, so with a sum of money exceeding two weeks wages in his hand to do with as he pleased, he felt like a millionaire. I remember the money was kept in a draw in the bedroom for some time, I don't recall what it was spent on, but I am sure it would have been spent wisely.

The village also had a concert party, where people of the village would carry out all sorts of acts. There was some serious singing by Mr. & Mrs. Gillet, together with musical instruments and comedy sketches. Mr. Waldock and Mr. Wilson once entertained us with a comedy version of 'Two Little Maids From School.' They had 'Girlie' masks on the back of their heads, and backs to the audience until the song ended, they then turned round revealing who they were.

Mr. Salter, who was Mrs. Waldock's brother-in-law entertained us with his Flute,

I think he was in the army, and could only appear when he was on leave.

Mr. Ron. Howes played the piano accordion on occasion. He was married to one of Mrs. Rubin Dellar's daughters, Betty, and he owned a shoe repair and sales shop in Huntingdon. Mr. Sutton who was a visitor to the village, entertained us with some monologues. I think he was in lodgings with the Grice family at Denmark House, and he was a representative for the Milk Marketing Board.

There were several other acts, but I can't remember them all.

Once I was the stage hand. This meant that I had the job of opening and closing the curtain at the beginning and end of each performance.

When I was playing at a whist drive, (I played the game from about the age of ten having had lots of experience at home), at the end of a hand of which I had taken the trick, I had the remaining three master trumps, which I laid on the table, saying, 'the last three tricks are ours.' Opposite me was old Mr. Moon, who objected to this and made me pick the cards up and play the game right out. My action of claiming the three tricks was normal play, but then I was only a boy!

To help out with the finances my Mother had a variety of jobs, none of them well paid of cause. One job was cleaning for a well known business family in Huntingdon She was known to the family, as one member lived in our village.

She had been working there for some time. One day the dining room was to be cleaned. This room had an open fireplace and was in regular use, so to clean it things had to be moved. On moving the wooden fender, Mother discovered a half crown. Realizing this had been set as a trap to test her honesty she replaced it. When Mother was about to leave, the lady of the house asked her if she had moved the fender for cleaning, at which my mother replied 'Yes and I put your half crown back, and I won't be coming here again.'

Left: *My Grandfather taking a break in the harvest field. He is well into his late seventies and still working full time*

Below: *Ladies in the harvest field. Left to right: Mother, Mrs Gough, Mrs Wendholt (Wendy), Ida Bates and Kate Byford*

This is a 'potato spinner', when the leading blade has passed under the crop the two spinning tines that turn inwards leave the potatoes in a row ready to pick up

Mother like many other women helped out with the harvest, usually Stooking (locally pronounced Stowking) That is standing the sheaves of corn up like tents so the air could pass through to help with the drying. After which the harvest would be carted to the farm yard and made into a stack, to be thrashed out later in the year or even into the next spring. Sometimes it would be thrashed out in the field where it was grown. This would mean getting the steam engine and the thrashing drum out into the field. Sometimes were employed contractors to make the straw into bales. There were no mobile automatic balers at the time, all the straw had to be man handled into a hopper at the head of the machine which was driven by a tractor via a large belt. The action was similar to the modern balers but the bales were held together with wires. These had to passed through a U shaped device from one side of the machine to the other, where another person would pass it back, completing a loop round the bail for tying off. These U shaped needles had to be placed accurately at two feet six inches intervals, which was the length of the finished bail. All the time the 'big dipper' would be cramming the straw into the ram for compressing. What ever would the health and safety people say now? If the straw was not baled on site it would be carted off to make a straw stack elsewhere on the farm for use as litter for the cattle yards. There was no straw burning in those days.

The same ladies that worked in the harvest fields also helped with the potato harvest.

Firstly with the planting, the furrows or 'stitches' as they were called, would be drawn out by a tractor and the stitching plough, three rows at a time. Earlier it would have been one row at a time with a horse drawn plough. I can just remember this method being used.

The seed potatoes were placed out in the field in sacks from which the planting team,(not all ladies), would transfer some into wicker baskets, to plant one at a time about ten inches apart, which was back breaking work!

When all three rows were planted the tractor would come along again. And the process would start all over again. When the tractor was on the return journey the same plough would split the stitches, so as to cover up the planted rows.

Stationary baler, the type that visited at Mr Jugging's farm. Note the 'U' shaped needles that determine the size of bales produced, also showing a Threshing Drum

In the autumn the whole process was reversed when lifting the potato harvest. This was done with a 'potato spinner' which took one row at a time. It had a flat shear that passed under the crop to lift the potatoes out of the ground, and then a spinning device shook off all the soil and laid them in a row ready for picking up. The same basket was used for putting them into sacks standing in the field.

When Mr. Gifford grew sugar-beet my parents would take on some of the hoeing. It was all done by hand. This entailed what was called 'chopping out and singling.'

The seed was sown in a continuous row. When it grew to about two inches high, it was too thick to grow into a mature plant, so it had to be chopped out to about six inches apart, this was usually carried out with a long handled hoe, that still left about six or so small plants, which had to be singled to leave only one plant occupying the six inch space. This was usually done with a small hand hoe, carried out by one's partner. This work was carried out outside normal working hours, at a piece rate, usually by the acre. This was just another way of earning a few extra shillings. Now in the twenty first century sugar-beet is sown with what is called a spacer drill, dropping only one seed every six inches.

Mother used to take in washing for the Americans stationed at R.A.F. Alconbury. She usually did it for three men at a time; any more would have meant too much work for her. Father said she should only take on two lots, but the loads weren't all that heavy, no uniforms or heavy clothing. The washing was brought round in a large American Army/ Air force lorry in big blue duffel bags. This was officially organized from the base and all had tags on with rank and name. We did meet the men as they had to collect their own bags. I remember one was a Captain, and another was a Sergeant, Mother called him 'Little Ted' because of his stature. George and I used to look in bottom of the bags to see if there was anything for us. Sometimes there would be a couple of oranges or some chewing gum. It was a punishable offence for any one to bring food off the base, so they couldn't bring goodies, cookies and the like.

The Americans really appreciated having their best shirt nicely ironed and folded, with a little starch in the collars. Ironing was probably the hardest part for Mother, as the old fashioned flat irons had to be heated on the trivet in front of the old range, one in use and one heating. Women's work was hard then.

About this time our neighbours changed a few times. When Fathers elder brother Charlie married he went to live in Huntingdon. He was married at Trinity Church, (no longer in existence.) Father's sisters were both married before Uncle Charlie, so this left Granny and Granddad and Fathers younger brother Jack in the big house, Lodge Farm. So they moved into the cottage 'round the corner' after Mrs. Cobley moved away.

Bill and Liz Cobley, no relation to our neighbour, moved from the end of Owl End into the railway carriage. Bill was well known for his excessive beer drinking, and was often very drunk, even though he couldn't afford it, but people would buy him the extra pint or two, knowing full well what the consequences would be.

On one occasion whilst still living in Owl End. Bill didn't get home, so Liz went looking for him. She got down the lane as far as Jim Brooker's house, knocking on his door and waking him up to ask if he had seen Bill. He told her that they had walked together as far as his house and that Bill carried on alone. They both went looking for Bill, and found him in the ditch, his legs on one side and his shoulders on the other, and his backside in the water, spark out! I don't recall how they got him home, but I am sure he would have had a good pasting with his own belt, as Liz was prone to do this I have been told.! Mr. & Mrs. Jim Cox moved into the cottage that Bill & Liz left, Jim also worked for Mr. Gifford. They had two daughters Barbara and Jean who is the younger.

The Bates family moved away from next door to us and were replaced by Mr. & Mrs. Elsom, they had a grown up family. Mr. Elsom worked on the farm along with two of his sons. The youngest of the family was Jimmy, and he was older than me, by about eight years. But we did have quite a lot of contact with him. Jimmy taught me how to use a catapult.

Aerodromes and Aircraft

The aerodrome at Alconbury. It is called this but it covered parts of Alconbury, Little Stukeley, Great Stukeley, and Abbots Ripton. I remember it being an R.A.F. Station at first. I can just remember the Stirling Bombers and the Wellingtons. Father sometimes used to take me to see them. The Americans took over in 1942. This is the year that George came to live with us, I was eight years old then, George is two and a half years older than me. The Americans had the Flying Fortress, and later the Super Fortress flying from there. We often used to go along to Little Stukeley to watch them take off. The runway then ran from east to west, the end of which was directly in front of the telephone exchange. We used to stand right under the planes, and we could see the rivets in the wings, there was no bank there then, when they went over us it made our stomachs churn.

Soon after the Americans came to Alconbury they put up a ring of lights round the base, about a mile from the perimeter. This was called the 'outer perimeter.' It consisted of a row of poles about sixteen feet above the ground with a light on the top with wire strung from pole to pole. There were about four or five of these in the field at the back of our house, but obviously they went right round the base. The holes for the poles were dug with a mechanical hole digger, no spade work for the Americans! The poles were fresh cut, with the bark striped off but no preservation treatment. I don't suppose they thought that they would be there for very long. One of the Americans was a ventriloquist and he had us bemused for some time, but one of his mates put us wise, and they all had a laugh about it. No doubt this was his party piece, and did it where ever he was. We had never heard of this art, not even the radio entertainers Peter Brough and Archie Andrews were known to us at that time, Archie being the dummy.

The Americans installed an outer ring of anti aircraft machine gun positions at various points. One of these was in the field next to where Jim Cox lived at the top of Owl End, which we often visited. Along with the gun emplacement was the ammunition stores, sleeping quarters and mess room; all thoroughly investigated after the war, a good play area. George had gone back to London immediately after the war, so this was one thing that we didn't do together. But like general McArthur. He will return.

When we were ready for school it was about the time the bombers were taking off to fly to Germany, we used to try to count them when they were circling over head to form up into squadrons. Sometimes we would see other planes from other nearby bases forming up with them. There were several aerodromes quite close. Three of these were American Kimbolton, Molesworth and Little Staughton, known as Staughton Moor. The Liberator bombers were at these bases. There were a few more American bases in our area as well.

When we came home from school the planes would be coming home, so we also took time to observe the return flight. We would see some of the planes were damaged. Some with tails nearly shot away, engines feathered, parts of wings shot off, holes in the fuselage and sometimes gun turrets missing. We realized as we became older and had a better understanding of things, that it was almost a miracle that they got back at all.

There was a Satellite base at Connington near Sawtry, where the planes flew straight to if they couldn't circle and land normally. There they would (Belly Land). That is with no under carriage, or maybe only one wheel down, this was done so that the other aircraft could get down in the normal landing procedure at the other bases.

Soon after the Americans were home to Alconbury in the afternoon, it was time for the R.A.F. to carry out their missions over Germany. There were several R.A.F. aerodromes close to us, the nearest of these were, Wyton, Warboys and Upwood, all fully operational and in a radius of about five miles of each other.

We would watch as they took off and circled overhead, just as the Americans did.

R.A.F. planes were mainly four engine Lancaster Bombers, although earlier there was the old Stirling, but they were well out of date. There was the two engine Wellington, a sturdy plane of the Barns Wallace design, which was still operational. There was also another four engine bomber called The Lincoln, this was a slightly lighter built aeroplane than the Lancaster Although these planes took off in the early evening, we could see them even in the winter because we didn't only have 'British Summer Time' but 'British Double Summer Time' This meant that the clocks were put back by two hours. Thus at six 'o clock in the evening time by the sun it was only four o'clock by the clock. This was also called daylight saving time. This allowed munitions and other factories to work longer hours before carrying out 'Blackout Procedures'

Also based at R.A.F. Wyton there was the 'Pathfinder Squadron.' The aircraft carrying out these duties was the 'Mosquito'. This was a light weight two engine fighter/bomber, built mainly of plywood. A very versatile machine, as fast as the spitfire fighter plane, and was used in varied roles. In its pathfinder role it would fly well ahead of the main bomber force, dropping flares of various colours as markers for the bomb aimers in the following wave of bombers. The Mosquito boys would probably have flown over the area two or three days previously on a photographic mission, picking out the targets for the bombers. These planes often flew unarmed on such excursions, making the plane lighter, with room for reconnaissance equipment. Early on in the war the Germans had no fighter planes that could catch them.

The Black Out meant that all windows had to be Blacked Out so that no light could be seen from outside. This was in case the Germans could see where the houses and other buildings were when they flew over. The actual material was supplied by the government, and was a jet black cotton type of cloth which had to be fitted onto frames, the responsibility of this was down to the house holder, my father made ours with wood which he like the other men were able to cut up on the farm saw bench, I suppose the wood was supplied from the farm. My father had quite a job to make ours as the windows were not very square, and the walls were uneven, but he was quite a clever man at this sort of thing. 'Put That B Light Out', was a catch phrase at the time.

One day when George and I were outside the house watching a Wellington Bomber and a Spitfire practicing attacking action, the Spitfire crashed into the Wellington, cutting the tail section right off, and itself breaking in half. We saw a parachute open from the Spitfire, but we never did know the outcome of this. We knew where the Wellington would have gone down, with all our knowledge of the area for miles around. So, we got on our bikes, road down to the farm and over the railway bridge at Lodge Farm and out onto the Abbots Ripton road. We were spot on with our calculations as to where it would land. But by the time we got there the road had been closed off, but we were able to get within about four hundred yard or so of the site. The main fuselage of the Wellington was in a small copse called Bellamys Grove, which is situated on the roadside, and the Spitfire engine was in an adjacent field. The rest of it was in several other locations, but not near the road.

On another occasion, we were playing on the bank of a dry ditch near to our house, when there was a terrific explosion, the ground shook so much that two of us fell into the ditch. Once again with our local knowledge we knew exactly where it was and the probable cause, as there had been no air raid warning. So we got on our bikes again, and went off to Little Stukeley. When we reached the perimeter of the airdrome we saw several Super Fortress Bombers broken up and scattered in pieces, one in particular sticks in my mind, it was standing on its tail resting on a building. We learned later that a bomb had exploded whilst being loaded on to one of the bombers, which is what we thought from the start, as we had watched them from the road on several occasions. The bombers would be lined up quite closely and the bombs would be on several small trailers, (Bomb Trolleys). Towed along with a tractor, like a small train, and then loaded on to the planes in turn.

Another explosion we felt was when we were at the Grand Cinema one Saturday afternoon, it shook the building quite badly, it felt a little more scary as we were all inside and in the dark. On leaving the cinema and on our way home we discovered that a petrol tank had exploded at 'Chalkie Whites Garage. Adjacent to The Iron Bridge. The buildings were badly damaged but I don't recall any person being hurt.

Another event that affected us slightly was one Saturday evening. We had been at The Three Horseshoes, that is, Mother and Father George and myself. Father like many other men enjoyed his Saturday pint and a game of darts. Mother had never been into a public house until the war, but Father wouldn't leave her on her own.

George and I, and other children were allowed to sit in a passage way between the main rooms, as this was not part of the licensed area. Licensing laws were a bit tighter then and children weren't allowed in the bars. But Mother mostly sat with us. A glass of lemonade and a packet of crisps was a night out. There had been an air raid warning, but that didn't seem to bother most people. The attitude was. If they are going to get us it doesn't matter if we are at home or having a pint. We had no effective air raid shelters anyway. When we left the pub it appeared as though the whole of the park and part of the village was on fire. What had happened was that the Germans had dropped a pattern of incendiary bombs, no doubt looking for the airfield, but had missed.

When we got home, this time going round the road instead of across the park, as it was on fire, we found that there had been an incendiary bomb just outside of our front door. Fortunately Mr. Wilson had seen this and had covered it with a bucket of sand, which was the recommended way of extinguishing this device; if he hadn't seen it we would have probably been homeless, as it had scorched the door. Mr. Wilson also managed to deal wither another bomb that had crashed through the roof of one of Mr. Charles Dellar's barns, thus averting another disaster. He did suffer burns to his hands, but not too seriously thank goodness.

There was one other local crash, this was when a member of the ground crew at Alconbury Base decided that he would steal an aircraft and fly home to America. The nearest he got to 'Home' was about three miles from the base. He crashed on the railway bank where the railway runs through Grange Farm; I think he was the only person on board.

***

George's parents used to buy us a whole range of comics, and send them to us once a month in a big roll, through the post. They included the Beano, Dandy, Film Fun, Radio Fun, Knockout, also The Hotspur, The Rover and The Adventure, these three were all full of stories, and George used to read them from cover to cover, I was not quite so keen on them. When they arrived we use to lay them all out and put them in lots for each week, then read them in order, and not mix them up. After we had finished with them we used to pass them on to others who were not quite as privileged in the availability of comics in our area. By the time village people had chance to get into town to the news agent, all would have been sold, as I believe there were restrictions on the amount of this sort of material issued. Save Paper was the slogan. Mr. & Mrs. Stillwell also used to save all their brass three penny pieces. And when they came to visit they brought them to us. They also brought us sweets, which were on ration, like most things during the war.

The Americans were very good to local children, in as much as they laid on Christmas Parties for us up on the base. This would usually entail a film show and party food, cakes and cookies and usually a gift when we left. The transport was provided. A big army lorry would collect us all up and then bring us all back again after the party. This in itself was an experience not to be missed. Just imagine about twenty or so children, with chaperones in the back of a lorry singing and shouting. We used to get American Red Cross Boxes. These were brought to the village school and handed out by Miss. Leppard. We had to share the contents, mostly one box between two children. Not a lot by to days standards, but we thought they were great. There would be glass marbles, chewing gum, cookies and other things that I can't recall, but they were appreciated, and we used to look forward to them.

George's parents lived in Bermondsey in London. They were bombed out twice during the blitz. Mr. Stillwell worked on the docks. This was one of the main targets for the German bombers, and the whole of the dock area took a regular hammering. But they didn't beat the Londoners spirit, even if their homes were knocked for six.

Mr. & Mrs. Stillwell used to visit when they could, this was difficult for Mr. Stillwell with the pressure of the job, often running for cover during the air raids, which were many, and then getting on with it again. The opportunity for time off was rare.

On one visit when Mrs. Stillwell was with us early or maybe the day before, when boarding the train at Kings Cross in the evening Mr. Stillwell wasn't aware that the train when stopping at Hitchin was divided. The front half going on to Peterborough, via. Huntingdon and the rear half on to Cambridge and the East. Of cause it was during the black out, and there were only minimal station lights, none at all if there was an air raid warning. He was on the wrong half and went on to Cambridge. Not only did he have his suit case, he also had a small sack of maize that he had swept off the dockside, about one stone, for my Mothers hens. He walked the whole way to Great Stukeley carrying both, about twenty two miles, arriving in the not so early hours of the morning. Some stamina! Even for a Docker. He would have been in serious trouble if he had been caught coming of the docks with the corn, even with that small amount. Pilfering was absolutely forbidden. They both enjoyed a day or two of peace and quiet in the country. Mr. Stillwell particularly enjoyed the atmosphere of the village pub, and liked to go with my Father up to 'The Local' for a pint.

My Grandfather also liked his glass of beer. He only went to the pub on Sunday lunch-times, I can remember quite clearly that he went every Sunday until he passed away at over eighty years of age. He always had the same, two pints of stout and home again. He, like all the others living at the top of Green End would go out the back of our houses across the field and up to the park. There was a hand gate into the park, across the designated path and out the other side to another hand gate. He always dressed the same, in his best suit. He only had the one, highly polished Sunday boots, probably hand made in those days. He most likely had them for years. He never wore shirts with collars, but always wore a 'Stock.' This a long narrow scarf type of neck wear folded from a rectangular shaped 'neckerchief.' This would be about two inches wide. It was passed twice around the neck, and tied at the front with a special flat knot. He was a smart old gent. If you see a picture of a 'Huntsman' he will be wearing the same type of stock. Grandfather also wore a large leather belt, not to keep his trousers up, but worn rather loosely, hanging downwards at the front round his well proportioned middle. He wasn't very tall, but broad and well rounded. He weighed a little over eighteen stones when he passed away at eighty three. The field at the back of our house was a grass meadow, and had a well worn track to the park, so no muddy boots.

George and I had what you call a good upbringing. There was no harsh discipline, just the requirement of respect and good manners, which come naturally when ones guardians have the same feelings for each other and other people.

Table manners were a must. No elbows on the table, all meals were taken at the table, correct use of your knife and fork, no talking with food in your mouth, not to speak at the table other than when necessary, no idle chit chat. 'There will be plenty of time for that when the meal is over.' Mother used to say. The table was not a place of silence by any means, if the conversation was kept to a minimum there was less chance of getting caught speaking with your mouth full, but if you did nothing was said, just a look from Mother. We always said yes please, and no thank you. Mother would sometimes say 'cut your food up smaller, don't put such large pieces in your mouth, chew your food properly.' It was no hardship to us, it all seemed so natural. There is no need to eat with your fingers while lounging in an easy chair at meal times is there? Which seems to be the trend these days.

We always had to ask to leave the table if we had finished before my parents. Sometimes Mother would say 'you boys can get down now.' When we had finished the evening meal Mother would enquire as to where we were going, and when we would be home. There were not many restrictions on us. In the winter she would say, 'don't go too far now, because it will soon be dark.' We were allowed out in the dark, and we liked it. Our imagination went further in the dark. As long as we stayed within ear shot of Mother calling us. And did she have a voice? I swear we have heard her at a miles distance. Other people use to remark on it, and they would say 'we heard you calling your boys.'

It didn't get dark until six o-clock instead of about four, as we had to be in by seven, we didn't get much of these 'dark games' Although as we got older the time we were allowed out got a bit longer.

One day when Mother was out working, we decided to have a spoon full of Golden Syrup. That would probably have gone unnoticed and would have been fine, but one spoon led to another and soon we had eaten about half of the tin, (a one pound tin), before realizing what we had done. We didn't say any thing, but it was only a few days before Mother discovered the half empty tin. Then we were in trouble, we owned up and apologized then got the lecture. When Father came home we told him what we had done. I can't recall the punishment was but it would have been pretty grim for us for a day or two. At least we would have thought so anyway. When this sort of thing happened, which I can honestly say was not very often. Mother didn't tell Father. We had to tell him ourselves, and that was punishment enough.

On another occasion, we stole one of Fathers cigarettes. Father smoked 'Woodbines' in the week or rolled his own, but for the week end he liked a 'John Player.' He would have these in a packet of ten, and keep them at home. And it was one of these that we took. If it had been a 'Woody' maybe he wouldn't have noticed, but the 'John Player' was Fathers little bit of luxury, so he rationed himself with these and knew just how many he had in the packet.

The treatment would have been similar to before. Just words, we didn't need any more than that.

Liz Cobley and the younger Mrs. Charlie Deller were both smokers. As cigarettes were in short supply they decided to have a go at rolling their own. One morning one of them went into Huntingdon and purchased some rolling tobacco and a packet of papers. When Father came home for his lunch, they had not managed to roll one between them. They had either torn the paper or it was too wet when they tried to stick it together.

I think Father said that they only had about ten papers left of the sixty in the packet, so he used the remaining papers and rolled cigarettes for the 'desperate' ladies.

At the end of our road 'Green End' there was a large advertising hoarding, this was about twelve feet wide and eight feet high, with a substantial support built with large timbers. One of our games was to climb up onto this and call out to people as they passed by. As we weren't visible from the ground people couldn't make out where the voices came from. Some would stop in their tracks and look around, puzzled or angry knowing someone was playing tricks on them. When we showed ourselves some people had a laugh about it, but some got quite annoyed. And would say things like, 'you frightened the wits out of me, boy.' Or 'it's a pity you haven't something better to do.' I don't think any one complained to my parents, otherwise we would have been told off. We thought it was good fun anyway.

An annual event was Rook Shooting. This was carried out every year on May the Twelfth, unless this was on a Sunday. This wasn't done for sport, but as a means of number control. Rooks were very numerous then and were classed as pest's, they caused severe crop damage if the numbers were too great. There were rooks nests in almost every tree in the long spinney, most of the larger trees in the park, and other pieces of woodland on the farm. The young rooks would just be able to fly, but not well enough to fly away when you approached them. There would be about four or five to each nest. This may seem cruel, but it was necessary. A flock of rooks could land on a field of freshly drilled wheat and follow the rows and eat the seed that had just been sown. A few well fed birds could soon mean the loss of one loaf of bread. They would also raid the crops when the corn was ripe. Mr. Gifford would invite other farmers to help with the control, usually Mr. Juggins and Roger, Mr. Bath from Hartford and his two sons Allan and Peter. Other farmers would be looking after their own shooting. Roger Juggins used to use a rifle, as did some of the others, but he also had a Four Ten shot gun which I used to carry for him. On occasions he would let me fire it. This is where I learned to shoot, including all the sportsmanship and safety. We boys were responsible for picking up the fallen birds, which often fell into the nettles, which were about two feet or more high, and did they sting! We also had to pick up the cartridge cases that had been fired. These were a hazard to the cattle that grazed the fields and the park. Cattle would pick the cartridges up and try to eat them, so this was as important as picking up he birds.

When the shooting was over all the birds were taken to the farm, here they would be tied in groups of six, and passed on to any one that worked on the farm. They were good to eat. Only the breast meat was used, Mother would cook the meat and then make a pie, with a nice pastry crust, a good supplement to the meat ration for a couple of days. There was no food wastage in the war time!

Rabbits were another food source for us. These would be caught in the winter, (Nov. to Feb) usually on alternate Saturdays, by the ferreting method, the holes where we thought the rabbits might be would have nets placed over them. Then the ferret would be introduced to one of the holes, and we would wait for results. The rabbits would bolt into the nets and were quickly dispatched, and the net replaced waiting for another rabbit to come to the same hole. There were usually four or five of us in the team, my uncle Jack, Doug and Brian Sewell, and myself. And sometimes my uncle Charlie came up from Huntingdon. We had free range of all the farm, as rabbits were plentiful. Some of the larger warrens would take us nearly the whole afternoon to work. We could catch as many as twenty in one day. The most we ever caught in one day was forty, but that was exceptional. Some of the catch would be left at the farm for Mr. Gifford to give to his friends. The rest my uncle would distribute amongst the other men on the farm, and ourselves.

The other times we caught rabbits was at harvest time. The crop then was cut with a Binder. This machine cut the corn just above the ground then tied it into sheaves and lay it out in rows. No combine harvesters then. The rabbits that were in the field would run away from the approaching machinery into the middle of the field, where the crop was still standing. When the cutting was almost complete the rabbits would make a run for it. Once out of the standing corn, they were mesmerized and didn't know where to run. Quite often they would try to hide under a sheaf where we boys were able to fall onto it and so catch the rabbit ourselves. We always chased them when they came out of the corn, sometimes even catching them as they ran round looking for somewhere to hide and would dispatch them as quickly as possible.

Rabbits made excellent eating, and we some times had it twice a week. Yet another good supplement to the meat ration. Much better than the sausages we used to get as there wasn't much meat in them! Like one of the comedians on the radio once said, there is so much bread in my sausages, 'I didn't know weather to put mustard or marmalade on them.' We even tried the whale meat sausages at one time.

It was war time after all, and I don't think that living in the country that we had it as hard as people living in the big towns.

Sometime before the air disasters I mentioned, our neighbours changed again. The Elsome family moved out and Mr. & Mrs. Vic. Clark moved in, with their grown up family. They moved from a farm in Wood Walton. Their children were, Brenda, Arthur, Louise, and Olive. Olive was the eldest, almost my Mothers age, and Brenda was the youngest, she was almost three years older than me, more Georges age. Brenda was with us when the Alconbury disaster happened, and was one that fell into the ditch. Mr. Clark came to work for Mr. Gifford as Cowman. He looked after the Milking cows calves, and the pigs, although there not many pigs on the farm, about twenty, I think.

There were one or two more moves in the village. One in particular was Mr. & Mrs. Gough. They moved from Moor Field Cottages up to The Old Rectory, and from there to Kitchener Terrace, all in about three years. The Gilbert family also moved away from Moor field cottages. When Mr.&. Mrs. Gough moved out of the old rectory Mrs. Gough's brother, Mr. Herbert Haynes and his wife Marjory moved in, they had a daughter called Elizabeth.

Although there were no real accidents with us youngsters, I recall George Gough having a nasty gash in his thigh, having come into contact with a barbed wire fence. I can remember his Aunt Madge taking him to the hospital on the back of her bicycle.

George also had the misfortune to get a bad electric shock. Down the cinder path was an electric pole with a guy wire support, we all did the same thing at one time or other. We would swing on the guy wire between it and the post. On this occasion there must have been a Short of some sort, and George was the unlucky one. It could have been any one of us boys. Another event that was funny to most of us, was when Derek Burton fell into the effluent side of the sewage works. These works are just between Great and Little Stukeley on the opposite side of the road to 'Cozen Hole.' I don't recall him being hurt, just rather smelly! Once when we were playing cricket in the park, on the official pitch, some one hit the ball towards David Brooker. He dived in an upward direction as though to catch it, but he didn't put his hands up in time and the ball hit him a nasty blow on the forehead leaving a large gash. It was almost as if he thought he was playing football and was trying to head the ball. Mr. Frank Cannon took him down to the hospital to get him sorted out.

On The Farm

Here I will try to recall all the men that were employed at Grange Farm. Not all of them will have been there at the same time. But most of them were there all through my boyhood and into my teen age years.

Mr. 'Dick' Deller, (there is that name again!) He was probably the first to retire. He always wore a bowler hat for work. I remember him most as the man that built the corn stacks when the harvest was brought home. He was often the butt of some jokes about his stacking. There would be three men on the stack. The first one would be under the elevator, this is the apparatus that carried the sheaves up onto the stack, after being placed into the hopper at the bottom. He would pass them to the second man, the first two men would be using pitch forks to pass the sheaves around, but the 'stacker' would use his hands to place the sheaves into position, binding them in as he went round the outside, while he was doing this the other men would be filling in the middle. The middle was always higher, slightly sloping outwards.

The jokes Mr. Deller had to put up with were things like. 'You have got it wider this end. You are not straight down this side. Wait a minute its falling over we will have to get some stack props,' and other such remarks; all in good humour. Building a stack is a highly skilled job, mostly set out by eye, or just paced with a marker. Most stacks would be built with rounded ends, whilst rising upwards it would also be widening out as well, until it reached the required height, then it would be drawn in at a sharper angle from all sides like a hip ended house roof. The size of the stack would have to be calculated to hold all the corn from one field or, one type of wheat. You couldn't have the stack incomplete and fill up with a different crop. This would cause problems when it was time to thrash out the stack. You can't mix corn varieties, nor would it be acceptable to not use up all the crop available and have some left over.

The above may seem to be a bit drawn out, but it does show that although farm work is mostly laborious, it is at most times very skilful. There was room for six large stacks in the Stack Yard. When the harvest was brought back to the farm and the stacks built they had to be thatched, not as thick as on a house, but enough to keep out the weather for one year. One or two men on the farm could do this job, my Father included.

When the stacks were thrashed out, the machine was drawn up along side the stack and fine mesh wire netting put up round the stack and machinery; this was to contain any rats and mice that had made their home in the stack. This is where us boys were employed again, not just George and me but one or two others also like George Gough and Lawrence Burton. We would each have a stick to dispatch the rodents as they tried to escape. We didn't have much chance of killing a rat, the farm dog was too quick for us, he was like greased lightening, just one bite and that was that.

We boys would dispatch as many as a hundred mice in a day from any one stack. One stack in particular was very infested with vermin. It was only a small stack but it had stood for two years at least, this is an exceptionally long time. It was in a field near to Owl End, close to the Hall Boundary wall. On the day all preparations were made prior to the machinery starting up. The stack was virtually heaving with life. We dispatched over four hundred mice from that small stack in one day.

Walter Gough, George Gough's Father worked at Grange Farm at this time, and he was another of the old timers, about twenty years older than my Father and had served in the first world war. Another old timer was 'Granddad' Clark. He was Vic Clark's Father and lived with him, next door to us. But like my Grandfather should have been retired years before, but they all wanted to do their bit, as old as they were. I remember him falling into a pond whilst cutting bushes, and coming home like a 'drowned rat' with scratches all down his face where he had fallen through the bushes, he had a really nice large white moustache, like an old colonel, about six inches across and curled at the ends, very smart, but when he came home it was all droopy, like the pictures of the Vikings. I think they stopped him from working after that episode. Like my Grandfather, they were both well over eighty when they finally retired.

When my Grandfather moved out of Lodge Farm Mr. Charlie Papworth moved in with his son and daughter. His son was called Ronald, he was quite a bit older than me and his daughter called Mary was even older. She was a nurse. I don't remember there being a Mrs. Papworth. Ron worked at the Grange, and Mr. Papworth looked after the cattle yards at the Lodge. Mr. Papworth had a straight 'peg leg', a bit like Long John Silver. He seemed to cope with it very well, and it didn't appear to interfere with his work.

We had a farm Blacksmith, Mr. Albert Bilby, he would carry out all the repairs to damaged or broken machinery. He could make tines for the various types of harrows from the metal parts for hand hoes etc. He could also make metal gate heads, hinges and the hangers that the gates swung on. In fact anything that could be forged. Even the holes in any parts he made or repaired were made while the metal was still red hot, with a punch and hammer. No electric drills were used then

To see two pieces of metal 'Forge Welded' is to see something very skilful indeed. The two parts have to be heated in the forge until white hot, but not burnt away, they would be placed on to each other on the anvil and struck in exactly the right place, usually only once for the smaller pieces. This of course was a two handed job, if my Father was around at the time he was usually the other pair of hands. Having had some experience in this trade, when he was a young man, striking for Mr. Boon of Chatteris.

After the welding, the piece could then be re-shaped to what ever was required. Just imagine making a chain by this method, Mr. Bilby could do it. Mr. Bilby made me a metal hoop, and a hook to run it with, this was just a piece of metal with a loop turned at the end. The idea was to place the hook on the hoop and run with it, but I couldn't manage this as I would hold it at the wrong angle, and often finish up with the hoop round my legs, and me on the ground, with skinned knees!

Mr. Bilby also carried out the farrier work, shoeing the horses; he always had horse shoes of all shapes and sizes to fit all the horses on the farm, which he made in readiness.

Mr. Bilby didn't live in our village, he lived in Abbots Ripton and cycled to work via Lodge Farm. He had a bicycle very similar to the one that the police man had, only Mr. Bilby had an old type of motorcycle seat on his, much more comfortable I would imagine. He left the farm, not retiring but moving to other employment.

In the next building to the blacksmiths was the farm carpenter, a much older gentleman, I think he was Grandfathers age. I never knew his real name but I remember his nick name was Tankie. He came from Hartford. He was a First World War veteran, and the name may signify that he was involved with tanks in that war. He was an excellent carpenter. I used to watch him when I could, I once saw him making a five barred gate, the main timbers would be cut on the big saw bench, I don't think he did this himself, although all the other work was. Every thing was done by hand, no mechanization at all. I saw him make a new shaft for a horse drawn cart with all the shapes and curves. Every thing that entailed any wood work he was the man, a lovely old gent who tolerated questions, even from a youngster, as long as it was sensible. He and Mr. Bilby often worked together on projects, the two trades went hand in hand, with both metal and wood being used on the same job.

My Grandfather could do most jobs on the farm. But not drive a tractor. When the drilling was being done he was the man who rode on the platform at the back of the drill, to make sure that the coulters didn't get blocked, or run out of seed.

The coulters are the tubes that the seeds run down into the soil, and if one of these got blocked with clusters of seed or, perhaps a piece of string off one of the sacks, it would show up when the crop emerged from the ground. So the drilling had to stop while it was cleared. Grandfather would often walk back down the row to see where the blockage had started. He would carry some seed in his hand and fill the row in. You could see quite clearly where part of a row was missing when the crop emerged if he didn't do this. More leg pulling. 'What were you doing, were you asleep? Look at that, you have missed half the field!' And other remarks! It was embarrassing if such mistakes could be seen from the road. The tractor driver would get the same treatment if the rows were not straight.

Grandfather also operated the dressing machine. This was a device for cleaning wheat and barley etc: to a very high standard. The grain was sieved and cleaned to a certain extent as it left the thrashing drum, but this wasn't good enough if the grain was going to be sold for seed. The dressing machine had a large fan which blew out all the dust and other small particles, with several screening trays where all the corn not up to the required size would be discarded and deposited into a sack, which would be hung under an outlet before the main collection point. This would be ground up and used for animal feed. The bulk of the corn was then carried along to the end of the process where it would fall into sacks, they were hung on a frame with two apertures, with a shutter opening the outlets alternately While one sack was filling the other one would be tied up and moved. These sacks were of a different class, made from a tightly woven hessian material, supplied by the corn merchant. These had the name Cadge and Coleman printed on them This company were often seen on the farm. They were a Peterborough firm. I can remember they used an old steam lorry for this work. I think it may have been a novelty really for advertising. It certainly made peoples heads turn when it was about. Otherwise, more often than not, they would be railway sacks, these were of a high quality, and hired from the L.N.E.R. These sacks were always used if the corn was being transported away from the farm. The same process was carried out for malting barley. This was sold to the brewery for making beer. Mr. Gifford supplied quite a lot of barley to the brewery in Huntingdon.

Grandfather worked on until he was turned eighty years of age, although when he was about seventy or so, he started work after breakfast, at nine thirty. He almost pleased himself what he did.

Mostly light work now, as one would imagine at that age, but he enjoyed working, rather than being at home with nothing to do, except get under Grandmothers feet.

Although not unheard of in the Fens, but rarer on the high land, My Grandfather, Father, and two Uncles all worked at the Grange at the same time. My uncle Charlie was older than my Father, and Uncle Jack, he was the baby of the family. Father and sons working together was common enough, but a Father and three sons is rare.

Uncle Charlie was a tractor driver. He left The Grange sometime during the war and went to work for Mr. Cullen at Hartford Hill Farm. This farm ran out of Hartford and up to the boundary of Wyton Aerodrome. One day when Uncle Charlie was ploughing in a large field close to the end of the main runway, he had a strange experience. It was a very foggy day, he said that if he hadn't started the day before and marked out his ground, he would never have been able to see where he was. When he turned at the top of the field to start his run down the hill, every thing seemed O.K. As this was a large field and ploughing is a slow job, and it took quite some time to complete a (round), this is up then down the full length of the field. When he arrived back at the top, there was an aircraft that had crashed just at the point he had left about twenty minutes earlier. There was no explosion or fire, the crash was about fifty yards short of the runway. The plane had probably run out of fuel, or missed the runway due to the fog when returning from a raid over Germany. I can't remember hearing about the crew, but a narrow escape for Uncle Charlie.

Billy Cobley was the horse keeper in my early years. Billy wasn't the most pleasant of men, or the best looking, he had a rather large nose and a screwed up face and spoke with a whining sort of voice. Maybe he was just old. This was at that time there was a mixture of horses and tractors, there were only about six horses then. But when my Grandfather started work for the Gifford family in 1928, he told me he had sometimes as many as sixteen to look after. This usually meant a really early start to his day, about four-o-clock. My father told me that that being out late, probably cycling home from as far away as Peterborough, usually with his mate Charlie Deller. He would sometimes be going up to bed when Grandfather was thinking about getting up. Father told me once he actually met Grandfather on the stairs. After coming home late from a dance

When Jim. Cox came to work at the Grange, he took over some of the duties from Billy who was about to retire. The horse was being phased out by this time and I can remember there being only three, by the time I was about eleven. One was a very quiet light weight mare named Kit. Then there was Punch a normal, sort of horse, probably a cross breed. Gilbert, he was a big horse, I suppose he would have been classed as a Shire, but he was white and there are no white Shires. He had previously worked on the railways somewhere up the north. Then there was Mr. Gifford's riding horse, which he used to ride around the farm on, keeping his eye on what was going on, and what needed doing.

Jimmie Lightfoot was a tractor driver and general farm worker, who lived in Huntingdon. Jim Byford joined the Grange when he came to Stukeley as an 'itinerant worker,' travelling round the country looking for work, I can remember him living in a little building just adjacent to the farm house. It had an open fire place, a table and chair, a big chair, and a bed what one might call, a bachelor pad. I think his meals were supplied from the farm house. He wasn't in this situation for long, as he married a local girl, Kate Robinson, who lived with her parents next to us when I was a baby. Jim didn't drive tractors; he helped with the stock cattle in the yards and other general duties. Mr. Ted Curtis told me that he too had come this way as an 'itinerant.' I can remember him showing me his bicycle hanging in his shed saying, 'He had come from Norfolk on it looking for work.' It was a racing cycle; he used another one for work.

Mr. 'Dick' Hobbs was the engine driver. This was a steam engine and it was used for driving the thrashing machine, both in the yard and when the thrashing was carried out in the harvest fields. The engine could pull both the thrashing machine and the elevator at the same time when moving around the farm. It was sometime after the war that the steam engine was sold. I believe a Mr. Edwards of Wood Walton bought it, and used it for demonstrations at country rallies and shows.

This steam engine is very similar to the one we had at Grange Farm

During the war there were three Latvian men. (Displaced Persons), living in Lodge Farm. They were victims of the war, their own country being over run by the Germans. All three worked on the farm at one time. One of them was married, his name was Tom he and his wife had a daughter Velta, who married a local boy and lives in Great Stukeley. Tom left the farm and set up home in Huntingdon and had a job in one of the factories. The other two stayed on the farm, and I think one of them died and is buried in Great Stukeley Church yard.

A team of Irish men used to come to the Grange for the sugar-beet harvest. First there was the 'Pulling and Knocking,' this means pulling the beet out of the ground by hand two at a time knocking them together to get the soil off laying them in rows with the tops of the beet level. Then one or two other men, depending on the size of the gang, would cut off the green top with a 'beet hook.' This is a tool much like a machete, but not cutting into the body of the beet. The more skilled men could do this without picking the beet up off the ground, hence the importance of having them lined up with heads level. If you had to pick the beet up to carry out this procedure, there was a fair chance you could chop your hand as this work was carried out at high speed.

Another group of men to work at the Grange were the Italian prisoners of war. They were billeted in a purpose built camp just on the Stukeley side of Huntingdon, where Knotley's Garage is now. They were timber buildings like large bungalows which the Italians kept quite smart. They tended the garden which they had developed themselves, with a rockery and, being Italian they had to have a statue which they were proud of. The Italian army had surrendered earlier on in the war, so things were not as strict with them. German prisoners had armed guards with them.

There were about ten Italians that came to the Grange, they came to help with the harvest.. After the war the Italian camp was made into accommodation for local people, I remember one of the families was Mr. Hall the Chimney Sweep, amongst others.

Sugarbeet waiting to be picked up, at the top end of Green End

Charlie Deller, Fathers long time mate, was also a tractor driver and general farm worker.

My uncle Jack was mainly a tractor driver, he my Father and Uncle Charlie, until he moved away to work for Mr. Cullen at Hartford Hill Farm, used to do all the ploughing when I was a lad. There was only the old type of Fordson tractors on the farm at this time, gradually improving as time went on. Uncle Jack did a lot of the engineering when specialist firms were not required. Father also used to do quite a bit of engineering and some forge work which he enjoyed. That was before any modern welding equipment was in use on the farm. Tractors soon became more abundant and varied. There was a John Deere which was almost like a tricycle, with the front wheels close together. This was mainly used for row crop work, using a piece of equipment that is mounted under the tractor, not towed behind, ideal for hoeing between the rows of sugar-beet and potatoes.

It made hoeing very accurate as it was able to get very close to the crop and cutting out the need for any hand work. The John Deere was a very versatile tractor and was Charlie Deller's pride and joy. Many others followed like Fordson Majors, Fowler Marshal, Ferguson, Massey Ferguson and an International Crawler. This was mainly used for ploughing and was Uncle Jack's tractor. Several more followed as the years passed by and all a little larger. My father, like most of the drivers could use all of them but usually each tractor had a designated driver. I remember when one new tractor came onto the farm; this was the first type of Fordson Major. This was produced to be an improvement on the Standard Fordson. It was not a particular good looking machine It had much larger wheels and was high off the ground.

When Mr. Gifford asked my Father's opinion of the new tractor, saying 'What do you think Arthur what do you think Arthur?', as this was one of his mannerisms. Father replied. 'It would do to block a hole in a hedge,' himself not liking the look of it. At this Mr. Gifford turned and walked off. After this episode, the new tractor was called 'The Hurdle'.

The Fowler Marshall was a strange type of tractor. It was a single cylinder diesel engine and when cold had to be started with a large cartridge that fitted into a socket in the cylinder head, this had a screw cap that fitted over the cartridge and had a firing pin that had to be struck with a hammer to fire the cartridge and so turn the engine over. Once the engine was hot it could be started in the usual way, by turning the engine with a cranking handle. This was Jimmy Lightfoot's tractor. This tractor was quite difficult to handle at times especially when turning at the end of a row when ploughing, there were no individual brakes to assist turning like modern tractors, and the front wheels were not always in good contact with the ground. I can remember on more than one occasion Jimmy finished up with the front wheels in the ditch.

Top: *(Standard) Fordson Tractor. Several models of this were made over the years, quite a few coming to Grange farm*
Bottom: *Fordson (Major), its doesn't look too bad here but when the first one was delivered to The Grange with iron wheels everyone thought how ugly compared to the old Standard model*

The International Harvester Co. 'T6' Tractor. It had a petrol/paraffin engine, not diesel. This was the first 'Crawler' type used at Grange farm

When this tractor was standing, and just ticking over, being a single cylinder it created a bouncy action and the driver would be jogged up and down, creating some mirth with onlookers. With the sound it made when running slowly, it was nicked named The Pop Pop.

The grey Ferguson, the first of this family, ran completely on petrol, most other tractors ran on paraffin, after being run on petrol until the engine was hot. The engine in this tractor was the same as the one used in the Standard Vanguard and the Triumph T.R. 4 motor cars, all being part of the Standard Motor Co.

The first tractor to be used at The Grange was an American 'Titan' this was made by the International Harvester Co. They were imported from America in about 1919 just after the 1914/1918 war. My Father drove this when he was a very young man. But it had gone long before my boyhood.

Top: *A 'Fowler Marshall' the type driven by Jimmy Lightfoot*

Bottom: *The little grey 'Ferguson' used by my father when he looked after the cattle*

Top: *A Gyrotiller for ripping out hedge rows and ditches*

A Titan tractor. The first tractor my father drove. First introduced into the country in about 1919 and already on Grange Farm

At one end of the farm yard, was an area called, the Ship Yard, this was where all the implements were stored when not in use. A lot of them were very old and were originally horse drawn, some of which had been modified to be used with a tractor. Others had been robbed as spares for other uses, probably modified to fit another implement. There was an old tractor there, it was an Emmerson, a name never heard of now, but this was not as old as the 'Titan.' George and I spent hours on this. We must have farmed The Grange all over several times.

Up until this time, a lot of hand work was carried out where nearly all the men had to turn their hands to jobs like, hedge trimming ditch cleaning, bank trimming, hoeing and cleaning out the cattle yards with forks. Sometimes the residue of continuously littering the yards with fresh straw would be as much as three feet deep, this would be carted off, by horse and cart in the early days, then with tractor and trailer to a point on the farm where it would be stored in a large heap for about three years, where it would rot down, eventually being used as fertilizer. This was carried out every year and the heap would be in a different place each time. This would then be carted out onto the fields and spread with forks onto the land, rotating the process so that all the fields would be fertilized about every two years or so. There were no artificial fertilizers then. Nor were there any sprays like insecticides or weed killers. The hoe was the weed killer! The only other form of fertilizer was a product called 'Fossit,' I don't know where the name came from, but it was imported from bird island. It was ground up bird droppings (guano) this was spread by hand early on, then with a Fertilizer Spreader, when farming became more mechanized. That was real organic farming. Another fertilizer was Soot, I don't know where this came from, probably from the industrial areas, factories and the like, but not locally. It was brought onto the farm in sacks, of what looked and felt like close woven cotton, so the soot didn't leak out. It was stored on the farm for a long time. I remember one large heap of soot being kept for so long that the sacks on the outside of the heap had rotted away, the soot didn't fall but stayed in the shape of the sacks. It had to be stored for a long time to allow it to mature and not be too hot, my Father explained that if it was used in its fresh state it would burn the crop when planted. This was used for Brussels other greens, and cabbages before planting.

There was another product very similar to soot. This was called 'Basic Slag' and came from iron foundries from under the furnaces. Both of these materials were used for the same purpose. These had to be used very early in the morning whilst the air was moist and dew on the ground. It was carried in a half moon shaped skip held waist height, with a strap round the neck, then strewn by hand on the ground, like the real old fashioned way of sowing corn. I remember my Father having to get up at about four o'clock in the morning to do this job. Some of the other men were also involved in this as it wasn't a one man job.

Mr. Gifford used to grow quite a lot of clover, the type with the red flower. This was sown at the same time as the wheat, and in the same drilling machine, the clover would be just emerging from the ground as the wheat crop was being harvested, this method was called 'under sowing' and was done like this because of the long time it took for the clover to germinate. The time to harvest the clover was when it had flowered and had 'gone to seed.' The farm still had an old fashioned 'reaper,' which had been modified from a horse drawn machine. It had wooden sails with wooden pegs in. The arms rotated and the pegs pulled the clover onto the cutter, then a conveyer belt laid it in a row. The old machine was used in preference to the modern type because the wooden sails didn't knock the seed out as the modern metal ones did. This task also had to be done very early while the dew was still on the ground and the seed heads had not opened. Again at about four o'clock in the morning. My Father did this job and used the Gray Ferguson which was very light weight. There was a seat on this old machine where another man would sit to make sure that the crop didn't get jammed on the conveyer, he had to be careful when moving about as the sails only just cleared his head.

Another crop grown on Grange Farm was Flax (Linseed). At the time it was a dual crop, the heads (seeds) were used for making linseed oil, but the main use was the straw, this was used for making real linen. It was not cut, but the whole plant had to be pulled out of the ground leaving the roots on. This was all done by hand, then tied into bundles ready to be collected. The straw at that time would be about two feet six inches long.

This like the red clover was grown for (the war effort). Linseed is still grown, but the straw has been reduced down to about eight inches. Only the seed is used now for making the oil, I believe it is only grown on small acreages. The fields that I have seen locally are usually about four to six acres. When in flower flax is a mass of very pretty light blue, but the flower isn't in bloom for very long.

The Stukeley side of Grange Farm ran parallel to Mr. Juggins Washingly Farm, along a farm roadway, which was known as 'Juggins' Roadway. This started at Washingly Farm and carried on over the railway to Sapley where Tesco's Supermarket is now.

Both farms had fields on that side of the railway. At The Spitals the lands ran parallel again. Most of this area is now used for industrial purposes, but some of it keeps the old names, like the Spitals and Blackstone, which is the name of one of Mr. Giffords fields. It used to be called Blackstone Leys. Also on this site there is a road called Washingly Road the name of Mr. Juggins' farm. All the fields on farms at that time had names, I can only remember a few of them. There was Long Mondays, Home Close, Horse Close, Stockings, Hundred acre, Forty Acre, Heron shores, Lord D's. Meadow, Lord D's Nine Acre, These were two fields belonging to Lord De. Ramsey of Abbots Ripton Estates, but weren't joined to any of his other property, and were rented to Grange Farm. There was Little Bonnets, Great Bonnets, Burnt Ground and a few others.

There were three railway bridges on the farms that I knew. Two were on Mr. Giffords farm. They were Lodge Bridge and Bonnets Bridge, the third one was on Mr. Juggins' ground, and is the one that is near the roundabout at Sapley. Bonnets Bridge, called

Gifford's Bridge on the ordnance survey maps, was dismantled when the railways were electrified.

My Fathers main job besides the normal ploughing, drilling harrowing and harvesting was to tend to all the outside cattle, that is the cattle not in the yards, although he looked after these in the winter. The outside cattle would graze most of the time from early spring up to autumn when the grass stopped growing, even during this period their keep would be subsidized if the grass was poor, with food such as mangle wurzels this is a root vegetable grown for cattle food, it was sliced up in a Mangle Grinder, before being fed to cattle, usually mixed with chaff or cut hay. Cabbages were also grown for cattle food, Father would chop these up a bit with a hedging hook. He would do this because cattle have only one set of teeth, and have difficulty in biting into any thing large.

I can't remember how many cattle there would be at any one time, but a large number were on rented land as well as on Mr. Gifford's own. One of the largest areas of rented land was the common that was owned by 'The Freemen' of Huntingdon. Part of this is now covered by Stukeley Meadows. This ground ran along the main road into town, opposite to the Spitals behind the then allotments, and until recently the bus depo. round to the water tower, then along the Hinchingbrook boundary bordering on to Mr. Raby's Brookfield Farm. I can't say what the acreage is but it was quite considerable.

Mr. Gifford also hired parts of Port Holme. On one occasion Father needed a vet to attend to one of the cattle. The vet in question was Mr. Hall whose surgery is in St. John's Street in Huntingdon. Father met Mr. Hall at the entrance and got him to sit on the back of the little gray Ferguson. Father knew the cattle would follow him thinking that it was feeding time. Father made a noose and held it on the end of his pitch fork, then slipped over the bullocks and held it until Mr. Hall attended to it. On returning to his car Mr. Hall said. 'Arthur that is the first time I have played cowboys since I was in short trousers'

Sometimes there would be a few on the grass land at the Spitals, this was only a small field and would only hold about ten or fifteen cattle, these would be cattle that had been segregated from the main herd for some reason or other.

Mr. Gifford also hired Stukeley Park for grazing. The field at the back of our house also had cattle in. In the main these cattle mentioned up to now were a mixed herd, predominately Herefords, but nonetheless a mixed bag.

In the fields closer to home was something quite different. A herd of 'White Belted Galloways' they were mainly black, but as the name might suggest they had a wide white band right round their middles. There was another herd of black cattle, these were also strain of Galloways, but not quite as large as the White Belted Variety.

Then there were the Black Aberdeen Angus, these were a smaller bread of cattle.

Not as big as the Herefords or Galloways. There was also a red variety, but Mr. Gifford's were the black ones. They were a more rounded shape and very fleshy, more docile and easy to handle. Father could always walk amongst his cattle and handle them with ease.

But the Angus was something else. They came to The Grange at about six or eight weeks old, and were kept in the yards until they were about six months old, there was about twelve of them. I don't know who was the biggest clown, Father or the cattle. He would hide tit bits of food about his clothing, and in his pockets, and these little cattle would jostle for position to find it, much like you would play with a dog, they sometimes knocked him down, I don't think he was ever trodden on, only on his feet at times.

He did love his cattle, and it was always a sad day for him when they had to go to market, especially the Angus, he had a particular liking for these. This bread were renowned for their quality of meat, although smaller they were always sought after at the market.

The meat was nicely marbled, so cooked much better.

Preparing cattle for market was the object of the exercise. It was a long process, and bullocks were at least three years old to be fully matured. The Angus matured a little earlier. The turn over rate depended on the size of the herd, not all cattle mature at the same time, and as they were generally bought in at about five to six weeks old you can see how one could get to know ones stock very well.

The Angus was the last type of cattle to be tried out at The Grange in my Fathers time. Not all the cattle were brought in for the winter, only the younger ones, most of them 'wintered out'

Not all the fore mentioned cattle were necessarily on the farm at the same time. Some of the special breads were not in place until after the war. The whole of this part of my memories is spread over a long period from young boy to late teenage and beyond. In fact my Father had just returned to the farm, from feeding the cattle on the common, when he died suddenly whilst talking to his brother Jack. He was not quite Fifty one.

During breaks in his education Macer, that is Mr. George Gifford's nephew, spent a lot of time with my Father learning about farming, ready to take over the Grange when the time came. Father always said that he was a nice enough lad but his heart wasn't really in it.

He wanted to be with horses all the time. He was an accomplished rider at a very young age, as was his elder brother Josh. They got this from their Father, Mr. Tom Gifford who so I was told, was more interested in horses than farming. Like Father like son.

Farming was a very busy occupation at all times. But one job seemed to have been carried out at a much faster rate, hay making. This was usually in June when the days were longer, and full advantage had to be made of this. In my early memories this was all labour intensive, and everyone on the farm had to join in. Firstly the cutting, this was done with a modified horse drawn cutter at that time, ours still had a seat on it where the man would sit whilst guiding the horse. Grass cutters didn't have a conveyor like the binder, the grass just ran off the back of the cutter and laid flat on the ground. This was left for one or two days, depending on the amount of sunshine we had. We seemed to have more then, didn't we? Once the hay began to dry out the men had to go along the rows, turning, and fluffing the hay so that the sun and air could get right into it. There would be as many as six men doing this. At that time the Grange didn't have a mechanical hay turner. After a few more days of sunshine the hay was ready for moving or stacking.

The men then turned the hay again making three rows into one, sometimes if it wasn't a very heavy crop they made it into small heaps, but mostly it was a good crop.

A stack was usually built in a corner of the same field. To get the hay to where the stack was going to be built, a hay sweep was used. This was a piece of equipment about ten feet wide made up of long wooden tines about six feet long placed at intervals of one foot apart fixed at the back end to a framework to hold them into position. These were made of knot free timber four inches square tapering down to about two inches with a cast iron point fitted over the ends turned up so as not to stick in the ground. This was mounted onto the front of a tractor and the hay was pushed, 'swept,' along the ground to the stack.

The first time I saw this it was mounted on an old Buick motor car. I used to get a ride in this. It was one of Mr. Josh Gifford's old ones. If there was any hay left in the field after the sweep had been used, a hay rake was used to collect up the odds and ends, the one at The Grange was horse drawn, and Kit the light mare was used for this. When the stack had been standing for a while, a sample was taken from the middle, to see weather it was getting hot, this sometimes happened if there was moisture in the hay when being stacked.

If it was getting hot, holes had to be burrowed to let air flow through. Hay stacks were known to burst into flame, this is called spontaneous combustion. The sample was taken by inserting a 'needle' into the stack and drawing a sample out. The 'needle' was a stainless steel rod about one inch thick, and three feet long pointed and with a barb on one side, like a harpoon, this was screwed onto a longer rod about six or eight feet long, then pushed into the middle of the stack, turning slightly then withdrawing, the barb pulling a sample out for inspection. If the hay was to be sold, the buyer would do this before agreeing a price on the quality of the hay. If the 'needle' came off the rod, it would be lost until the stack was used. This is where the saying. Looking for a needle in a hay stack came from. The hay was stored until winter, then it was used to feed the cattle, because hay settles down and consolidates, the stack can't be opened up like straw. Hay had to be cut, using a large bladed knife, it is called a stack knife. This blade was two feet long and six inches wide but very thin like a scythe. It has a 'T' handle and is used with a slicing or a sawing action, cutting the hay into slabs, working ones way down the stack in steps. This method slowly came to an end when the modern machines came into use, grass cutters, hay turners and especially balers.

A Hay Sweep mounted on a tractor Not on the old Buick motor that I can remember

This is the type of tractor and plough my father let me drive on my own

There were a few visiting contractors to the farm. The steam ploughing team were the earliest that I can remember. There were two large steam engines, and a really big implement that was a double ended plough. It had twelve bodies each end. Whilst one side was being pulled along in one direction the other half would be sticking up in the air.

When it reached the end of the field, the opposite end would be lowered ready for the return journey. The plough worked about ten feet each time it crossed the field, it was attached to a heavy cable which was on large drums under the engines. When the right end engine was pulling, the left hand one would be releasing.

There was a 'steersman' on the plough just to keep it straight. Every time the plough reached the end of the run the engines had to move up the amount that had been ploughed, ready for the next pull. The engine drivers would signal to each other with the steam whistles, telling when to start pulling or stop. They would whistle up the water cart, which was always at hand close to where the work was being done. There were several combinations of calls, with different amounts of whistle blasts, and length of blasts. It was fascinating to watch and listen to.

Another visitor was the 'Girotiller' This was a large machine on tracks that had a large round cultivator, about five feet in diameter with tines of about two feet six inches long. This had a rotating action and was used to rip out hedges, and stir up rough ground to make larger fields, so as to grow more food all for the war effort. This was on the instructions of the government

There was also a 'Dragline' that was the forerunner of the modern J.C.B. type of machine. It was operated with wire cables, unlike the modern ones, which are all hydraulic now. This machine came to clear out all the ponds, and make them deeper, but with a shallow end for cattle access to drink. This was operated by two Land Army girls.

This also was a government requirement. Sometimes we would get a ride on this, and watch all the operations that were carried out with the multiple leavers. They were very good at their job. This was done the year Father won the beer at the bowling for a'Pig,'

I remember the girls coming in for a glass of Arthur's beer.

A reaper similar to the one at Grange farm

When George and I were out and about, during our school holidays and week ends, there was never a dull moment. We learnt a lot about nature, the way farming was carried out, all the different crops, when they were planted and harvested at various times. When the different trees came into leaf, and the shapes of the leaves, and the fruit they bore, horse chestnuts, acorns and beech mast, these two could be collected for pig food. Wild roses gave us rose hips that were gathered and passed on to either W.V.S. or the Red Cross. We all had a go at this. It was organized through the school. We were told they went to make Rose Hip Syrup, for children in hospital, I tried it and it was very good. On hawthorn the fruit were haws, a little red berry with not much flesh and a stone inside, not much nourishment. The birds did take them in severe winters. The blackthorn produced sloes, a very dark small fruit of a damson colour. These stayed on the bushes right through the winter. Not for the birds as they are very bitter to taste, but ideal for making 'Sloe Gin.' There are lots of wonderful things to see in the country that we take for granted, but a lot of people in the larger towns didn't have the chance to see. A lot of children coming from London didn't know where milk came from, having never seen a cow. But once they got into the country they soon learnt about nature. Things like catkins on the willow trees, cob nuts (Filberts) on the little nut trees in Prestly Wood, chestnut trees bursting out in flower, like huge candelabra. Cowslips in the meadows, primroses on the dyke banks and along the railway line, violets on the outside of the spinney, bluebells on the inside, so much more to see if only one took the time.

We saw things like chickens being hatched, calves suckling on the cow, little pigs suckling, all in a row sometimes as many as ten. I had even seen a calf being born by the time I was ten. It is all about nature and farming, and gives one a better insight to life later on. I don't think it did us any harm to know about this sort of thing at that age. It all seemed so normal to me being brought up so close to nature.

We used to see if we could find a Swede in the mangle field, this was a regular happening there would often be quite a few, the men would look out for them when harvesting the main crop, they make a very nice vegetable, and are grown commercially now for the super markets.

When we were on our expeditions, we seldom had any drink with us as unless there was a severe drought, as we could always get a drink from the land drains, these were clay pipes about two feet deep under the soil and ran into the main ditches.

Some of these drains had been in the ground for up to two hundred years. As there were no chemicals used in farming at that time, as long as the water was running clear it was considered safe to drink. When we were at home we drank from the well. There was one ditch in particular that was really good, it was so pure that water cress grew there, it ran over a nice gravel bed and was as clear as gin. Father had told us that if the water cress grew there, you would come to no harm from drinking it.

During this time I used to spend as much time as I could with my Father on the farm, I was interested in all things to do with the farm, especially the tractors. When Father was ploughing he would let me drive the tractor on my own, that would be at the age of eleven or so, he would get off and make a fire, for toasting our sandwiches.

He would start me off and I would carry on by myself for a few rounds. The tractor was an old type of Fordson, with a two furrow plough; this was a trailer plough not like the modern mounted ones. At the end of each row you had to pull a cord to lift the plough out of the ground whilst still travelling, and after turning in at the start of the next row you had to pull the cord again to drop the plough in. All this had to be carried out whilst still moving, and one had to be accurate with the lifting and lowering to keep the rows in line, otherwise it made it difficult when finishing off the field.

It is called ploughing the headlands. If the start and finish of the rows in the main runs weren't in line, it would mean that you would plough over the ends twice, making it difficult to make a good finish. All ploughmen were proud of their work, and if it looked a bit ragged at the end of the job they would be disappointed..

A pair of steam 'Ploughing Engines' similar to the type that used to visit Grange Farm. Note the cable drum on the underside

106

I used to go on trips with Father to Huntingdon to deliver barley to the brewery malt house; this was situated in St. Johns Street. The brewery owned quite a lot of buildings there, mostly backing onto Chivers on the west side of the street, but also a few on the east side next to St. Johns Cemetery with a walk way over head and a conveyer for the grain. The barley was in large sacks,(usually Railway Sacks) and were hoisted up to the top of the building with a chain that Father used to fit round the top of the sacks. They would then disappear through a trap door that hung out over the road with a little roof over it. Father always received a glass of beer on these trips. He said that it was far better than the beer at the pub. One part of the old brewery property in Saint Johns Street still exists. That is the Maltsters House, and is a listed building. It is now the head quarters for the Hunts F.A. The main brewery was in the High Street. This covered a large area and ran parallel to Saint Germain Street down one side, to what was at that time Wood & Ingram's nursery. The frontage went almost up to Trinity Church opposite to Fishers & The Hippodrome Cinema.

While on the farm with Father he would point out all sorts of interesting things, like where there was a pheasant's nest. He knew where a fox had been and pointed out the smell of a dog fox if he had passed that way in the night, and where he had made a kill.

At the back of the farm yard there was a gate leading into the fields, and on the gate post someone had fixed an old binder tool box, that had a hole in the bottom, and every year a tit built in it. George and me were allowed to look in the box and see the nest, but only once a year. All the men knew of this nest, but I don't think any other boys were told about it. None of the other men had sons, it was only George and myself that were about the farm at that time. Once we had our look, it was 'now you have seen in the box, leave it alone and don't disturb the bird.' Likewise any other nest Father showed us.

I learned about all the crops on the farm, when they were sown and when they were harvested and what they were used for, also all the implements. As time went on the implements became more sophisticated. With the old drills the amount of seed put into the ground was determined by the size if the cups which were on the spindle that ran through the seed box. A lot of this would have been guess work as there were only two sizes of cups on most drills. When the new type of drill came into operation the amount of seed per acre was determined by a more accurate method. This amounted to a series of interchangeable gears mounted into the mechanism that was driven via the main wheels. There was a chart issued by the manufacture as to the combination of the gears to use for any given seed, from the smallest, like clover through all varieties of grain, and onto the larger seed like peas and beans, thus not wasting seed by over distribution.

After some time the operator, my Father, got so used to the combinations he did not need the chart when changing crops. My father was usually given any new machinery to try out and to learn all about the operation. My uncle Jack got new tractors to try out. Father and Uncle Jack carried out most of the repairs on the farm machinery and tractors. With ever increasing modernization, the workers on the land began to lose the Farm Labourer label, and became agricultural workers. The drill (circa 1946/7) would now be a museum piece. Agricultural machinery and implements are becoming more and more sophisticated, most specialized machines are computerized now.

Along with all the normal working of the crops Father still had the cattle to attend to. He told me all about the different breads, and things that could go wrong if they weren't cared for properly, he had a good eye for that and could spot any thing out of the ordinary straight away. If he thought it necessary he would ask for the vet to come and have a look. When I was very young, about five or six, there was a large Hereford Bull on the farm, his name was Tom he was kept on the lodge farm, there were always a few cattle there, Father would sit me on his back sometimes, he was very tame. Mother was not well pleased, and said that Father ought not to do such things, as you could never trust a bull. He still put me up on him even after this. But Mother didn't know.

Lots of other things were happening on the farm, always something different going on.

One day I was with Mother outside the Grange Farm house, when the farm terrier bit me on my ankle, when I held my leg up to tell her the dog has bitten me, he immediately bit me on my other leg. Neither of the bites were serious, no more than a scratch I suppose, but Miss Cooper put a bandage on my ankle, the dog wasn't punished, only shouted at, I had probably trodden on his foot or something.

Another incident was when Ron Papworth who lived at the lodge, was either putting a horse into or out of a cart, when the cart ran forward and the shaft went straight between Ron's legs. Very painful! Someone took him round to the house to see Miss Cooper who immediately had his trousers down, while she helped Ron by holding him under the pump outside the back door. The man that took him round operated the pump. I was there at the time. Ron had left school by then and had started work on the farm, I would have been about eleven, but I was always round the farm, and didn't miss much that went on. One day Father asked me to collect his wages for him, which I had done before.

He was probably working late at the Spitals or somewhere like that. Wages were always paid out on Fridays at five o'clock. I arrived at about a quarter to five and Mr. Gifford opened the kitchen door. Laid out on the table in little lots were each mans wages, and a big ledger with all the details in it. On seeing me he said, 'What do you want?' When I said that I had come for Fathers wages, he said 'You wait till all the men have been.'

At the time there were no other men in sight. So he was just being awkward.

Mr. Gifford had another brother, Tom who farmed at Little Stukeley. He also had those large bushy eyebrows, I think even more pronounced than his two brothers. Mr. & Mrs. Tom had three children. Josh was the oldest, named after his Grandfather, Macer and Susan. Both Josh and Macer were well known National Hunt jockeys, Josh being the more successful, and better known. He went on to be a very successful trainer.

These three eventually inherited both The Grange and Lodge Farm, Josh and Macer getting The Grange and Susan getting The

Lodge. I was given to understand that Mr. George said that the two farms should be separated on his death.

Macer lived at The Grange, but Josh lived away, concentrating on his horse training business, he wasn't really interested in the farm. Macer tragically died at an early age. Of Motor Neuron. He was forty one. Soon after this Josh sold the Grange, and carried on with his training. Susan still has The Lodge.

Sitting on Mr. Deller's fence with my bandaged ankle after the farm dog had bitten me.

School picture with my Cub's neckerchief

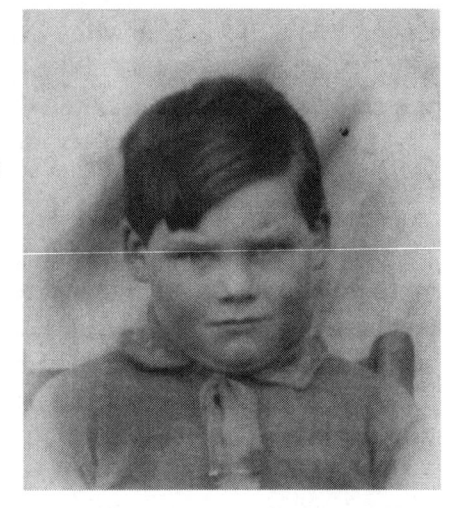

Home Grown

Like nearly all village people we had a fair sized garden where Father grew garden produce through the seasons. There was an old orchard near to our houses that had probably been there since the old house was built. So when the call came to 'Dig For Victory' My Father, Uncle Jack And Mr. Vic Clark, our neighbour, decided to open up gardens in the old orchard. Breaking new ground, a back breaking job! They weren't afraid of hard work and had done it all their lives. George and I had our own little plots. We grew plants like cabbage, brussels and that sort of thing from seed, so that Father was able to plant them out in the main plot later on.

Grandfather kept two pigs in a sty, in the orchard. When the pigs were well grown, and fattened I do mean fatted not like the modern razor backed skinny ribbed things we see today. One pig had to be given up for some government scheme or other. Home kept pigs had to be registered at that time.

The other one would be butchered and returned to Grandfather, which he shared amongst the family. That meant home made sausages for a meal or two. Lard, which was the pork fat rendered down at home, it was cut into cubes about one inch square then placed into a large pan and heated until the fat had been run off. The temperature had to be just right, not to hot or the fat would burn. The residue from this procedure we called 'fritters,' much like Pork Scratchings today, but much better, with a lovely crunchy honey comb texture. The hams were home cured, as were the shoulders. One side for bacon, the rest was for fresh pork, we had no refrigerators, so it had to be salted or dried. The down side of all this was that those involved had to give up part of their meat ration.

Mother kept hens, and had done all her life, but any one keeping six or more hens had to register with the ministry of food, and had to give up the egg ration for the family.

Mother had about a dozen or more hens at a time, although they didn't all lay at the same time. How lucky we were living in the country then..

Mother mostly bought her hens as 'about to lay pullets,' but some times she would have a hen incubate some of her own. There was always a cockerel in with the hens, so one could be fairly sure that the eggs were fertile. We also had a few ducks and a drake. Mother some times would sit a hen on duck eggs, hens were generally better sitters.

When the eggs hatched, there was immediate bonding with hen and ducklings. But the natural instinct of the ducklings was to find water. We had a small pond for the other ducks so they had no difficulty there. It was a strange sight to see a hen pacing up and down the waters edge trying to call her 'chicks' off the water.

***

During the war we still had the normal tradesmen call. I well remember them.

When Mr. Crowe gave up the milk round from his own cows We had Joe Turton delivering milk. I think it was for the COOP. He has a hand cart with two large wheels and shaft like handles. The milk bottles were in crates.

Glass was in short supply and Joe was not supposed to leave any milk without collecting the same amount of empty bottles.

He had a regular call. No B*!*!y Bottles No B*!*!y Milk, but I don't think he left anyone without milk. He could always collect them the next day.

Joe suffered with a stomach condition, and one could follow his rout round the village like a paper chase, there was a trail of little green and white squares of paper, the wrappers off his indigestion tablets.

Mothers bottles were always washed out and left on the door step, she always kept our milk in a jug, Mother would never have a milk bottle on the table.

Our butcher came up from Huntingdon, I think the name was Ayres. He had the shop on the corner of George Street and the High Street It was a butchers for many years, changing owners several times. It is now a Bookmakers.

Our baker came from Godmanchester. He was Mr. Oxborough, and like the butcher he employed a rounds man. We always thought his bread was better than most, it was nice and crusty, and didn't fall apart when it was cut.

Mother always bought her groceries from The International Stores in Huntingdon, either walked to and from town, or sometimes on her bicycle. She mostly shopped on Saturdays. The 'International' had a brand name for its own goods, which was 'Mitre' products. And the symbol was a bishop's head dress. The shop was opposite the market square and is now a Savers Store.

George and I would go with her and help with the bags, not that there was much to carry just the bare essentials, not many luxuries around then. But always with the ration books at the ready, as everything was 'On Ration.'

Father always got the tea ready on Saturdays, except in harvest time, ready for Mothers return from the shops. We mostly had fish or meat paste sandwiches and then perhaps one round of jam instead of cake. We always had a cooked dinner on Saturdays and Sundays, the rest of the week we had the main meal in the evening.

Another baker that came to the village was the COOP. They had a horse drawn bakers van. The rounds man was not particular as to where his horse might be.

He often left it outside a house where he had a cup of tea, or chatting, and the horse would wander off. Often just grazing or taking a nibble at some ones hedge with the cart diagonally across the lane, which was not very wide. People had to move him on so that they could get past, often swearing about Ben and his B horse.

We had an insurance man, like most families did; ours was Mr. Barker from Huntingdon. The company he represented was the Liverpool Victoria he was a well known and well liked man. He had a brother also well known in Huntingdon, who had a window cleaning business, and could be seen on most days cleaning the big shop windows.

Mother also had a man call who sold clothing He came from Peterborough and had a little Morris eight motor car. He was Horace Hill a popular tally man, payment was made on a weekly basis. His customers had a card that he would mark off for each payment made. For all the regular callers Mother would set aside all the monies. Always the correct amount in separate piles under the piano lid, so that when they called the money was always on hand. There was another regular caller, Ron Colman, known as the accumulator man. With the old battery radio's you had to have another small device called an accumulator. This was an electrical gadget with terminals like a battery, but was made of glass and you could see the acid inside. These had to be recharged, usually once a week. Ron would collect these, bringing another one as replacement and take the run down one for recharging. I think it cost sixpence for this service.

During the war years everyone had to have an identity card. Unfortunately Mother managed to lose hers and mine. What a performance, the police had to be informed of the loss, and of course the government department that dealt with it. There were forms to be filled in as to where, when, why, and how they had been lost, and questions from visiting officials. Witnesses had to be contacted to sign the forms. A Doctor, JP or a person of standing would have to vouch for you. I didn't understand at the time how upsetting it was for Mother. She felt she was being treated like a criminal. Neither Mother nor I were allowed to forget the event, as the original cards were Grey and the new ones were Pink, showing that they were replacements. They stayed like that until the system was abandoned. I knew later on in life that Mother always felt stigmatized by this. We had a gas mask in a little square cardboard box with a carrying strap, that we were supposed to take it with us every where we went.

George and I used to have our hair cut at a barber shop at the north end of Huntingdon next door to Mr. & Mrs. Horner's Wet Fish & Green Grocers shop. The barber was Mr. Smith, Father took us for the first couple of times and then we went on our own. Mr. Smith was a well known character, though not necessarily the best barber in town. There were no electric hair clippers then, only hand ones, and I am sure they were not the sharpest.

He used to pull quite a lot. All the time he was cutting hair he would be whistling, well not so much whistling but plenty of blowing! When he wanted you to turn your head instead of just a gentle push left or right, he gave us a sharp jab with one knuckle just behind the eye. If you were unfortunate to be in the chair when his morning drink was due, it wasn't tea, but cocoa plus a large door step sandwich, which he consumed, with a 'slurp' whilst still cutting your hair and trying to whistle. Consequentially one got a shower of crumbs for free.

I continued to go into town with Mother on Saturdays now and again, especially if I wanted something for myself. But this fell of by the time I was twelve, as I had much more interesting things to do. I remember going into town to meet my Auntie Marjorie, Mothers Sister. We used to have coffee and a cream cake at Stiles the baker. Their shop was opposite the George Hotel, the bakery shop was on the ground floor and the restaurant upstairs. This was a real treat for a young lad The shop has changed hands several times since then. It has been an English and then Greek restaurant. At present it is a Charity shop. Next to Stiles shop was Claytons, they were harness and saddle makers. I used to go into here for my catapult elastic and air gun pellets. (George had sent me an air gun from London for my birthday.) They sold a whole host of goods, including sporting items. My Uncle Sonny, Mothers Brother, and Aunt Kath bought me a pair of Clamp On ice skates from here. Toys were also sold. My Meccano set was purchased from here. Mr. Moon's toys were sold from here during and after the war. This shop, like so many of the old shops at that end of town, is an estate agent now.

Mr. Clayton who owned the shop was a well known Huntingdon man, he was a town councillor, and had been the Mayor on occasions. He had an impediment in his speech, and I was told by an old man that knew him well when they were younger, that one day when he was addressing the scout troupe on the market square he allegedly said. 'When the dwum blows and the bugle goes watty tat twik march.'

***

At this time, early in 1944 there was a lot of military activity in our area. Almost every day on our way home from school we would see convoys of American Servicemen sometimes up to about twenty lorries. These men had been flown into Alconbury from America, to be dispersed around the country in preparation for the 'D' day invasion.

One day we had a surprise on our way home. In the park there were English Army Lorries about eighteen to twenty among the trees. They had come into the park by way of the gateway at the lodge,(Mrs. Deller's house). There were no soldiers, just the drivers, and escorts on motorcycles. We couldn't see inside the lorries as they were all sheeted down. I remember one of the drivers in particular; he had bright ginger hair and freckles. He asked if we had any spare food at home as they were hungry. On relating this to Mother she went to our food cupboard, and produced a loaf of bread which she cut in half and sent us back with one half for the boys.

In the early days of the war, on some nights we were allowed to stand outside with my Father and his friend Charlie Deller. to see in the distance how the sky was lit up from the bombing raids on London, which was only about sixty miles away as the crow flies. The conversation would be something like, 'I wonder how many poor people are homeless tonight' or 'how much more of this can they stand?'

We didn't know if George's parents had been Bombed Out again. This must have been early evening in the winter; otherwise we would have been in bed. No late nights for school boys then. Being only about seven or eight at the time I don't think that I fully understood what was going on, but I am sure that George did he being that much older than me.

On one of these evenings we saw a German bomber caught in a search light, probably from Wyton aerodrome, it seemed to be a single plane, possibly off course.

These actions may appear to be a little unwise now, but, Father, and other people, used to say that having no air raid shelter we were just as safe outside as being in the house. Having so many aerodromes close to us we were considered to be quite vulnerable to catching the odd stray bomb.

Two Great Stukeley young men saw the Germans drop bombs on the race coarse and surrounding fields. The two men were Russell Hobbs and one of the boys of Deller from Brookfield farm, on their way home from town. I think it would have been late evening. It was explained to us later on that the pilot had probably mistaken the jumps for aircraft on the ground, as it is only a stones throw from Alconbury base.

Quite a few Stukeley men were in the forces during the war, I can't remember them all going in, but I can recall most of them coming back. There was Stanley Hobbs, and his younger brother Russell, Basil Hayward and Charlie Hamilton were all in the Royal Navy. Another Hobbs boy, Roy was in the army, as were Ernest Cobley and Reg. Elsome. Geoffrey Wilson was drafted into the coal mines as a Bevin Boy, later to be in the army, serving in Italy at the end of the war. Maurice Walsh was in the R.A.F. as was Mr. 'Monty' Fenwick of Stukeley Hall, he was a Squadron Leader.

Unfortunately both Ernie Cobley and Reg. Elsome were killed. I think one of them was at Dunkirk. There is a person called Hanson, whose name is added to his parent's grave stone in the church yard as being lost in the war. I can't recall this first name.

My apologies to the persons or their families that I may have forgotten or missed out.

Landmarks Remembered. On the way to school

After leaving Green End, on our way to school we passed to our right the road to Mr. Raby's Brookfield Farm. Then down 'Spitals Hill,' On the left were the Alms Houses. Next to these were Mr. Juggins' Spitals buildings which included a large dutch barn and some other buildings one of which housed the sheep dip. On the left were the Spitals fields belonging to Mr. Gifford then a small farm belonging to 'Mexie' Saunders. The nick name for him came from his Father who years earlier sold goods such as, paraffin, grease, oil, and other products manufactured by 'Shell Mex' the petroleum company, he sold these from a horse drawn trolley. A little further down on the right was a small field with some buildings that belonged to Mr. Sid Smith, who had a small butchers shop in the north end of town. He had a 'Slaughterers License.' These activities were carried out in the buildings. This became Shakespeare Garage whose owner was agent for big American 'M.M.' Tractors.

On the left was a wooden bungalow and other buildings, owned by Mr. Doug Lamb, who was a well known local market gardener and green grocer, and had a stall on the Huntingdon market. He had quite a large portion of the allotments on the opposite side of the road to where he lived.

These allotments continued on behind the houses on the right hand side, backing on to the 'Freemen's Common.' Of the original houses on that side, only Alexander Place remains; all the others have been demolished and new ones been built. In one of the small houses that have gone, a Mr. & Mrs. Tom Day lived and ran a tobacconists shop. On the left hand side, the next buildings were the Italian P.O.W. Camp.

Where the Conservative head quarters are now, was a timber yard, which I think belonged to Spencer's, they had moved to that site from where the New Grammar school was, behind the railway station, opposite Hinchingbrook. I think in about 1935/6. On the right was the bus depot, and 'Chalkie' Whites garage.

.Passing under the Iron Bridge which carries the main L.N.E.R. railway, immediately on the left is Saint Peters Road. During the war there was a huge Static Water Tank here, this was for emergency use for the Fire Brigade, should we ever get bombed. This large tank was made up with steel panels bolted together, they were all of a uniform size about three feet square, a tank could be made to virtually any size with these. They were called 'Braithwate Tanks.' Some of these tanks can still be seen around the country side on steel frames.

On the corner of Saint Peters and Ermine Street was North End Garage, and a little behind this was the 'Union' as it was called then, in Victorian times it would have been The Workhouse. It had several nick names; one I remember was 'The Spike', Finishing up as a hospital. During our school days we could often see 'Gentlemen Of The Road' queuing up here for a nights lodgings, for which they would have to carry out some duties or chores.

On the left was Mr. Alfred (Alfie) Iron's shop, this was a very popular establishment.

He sold a wide range of products, from sweets, tobacco goods, grocery, and small items of hardware. Next to him was a shop owned and run by his sister Miss. Irons, she catered for all the ladies requirements, from knitting needles through to clothing.

On the left was a large open yard and buildings, this belonged to The Ministry Of Agriculture. Known as The War-ag. The yard contained machinery for land drainage and other agricultural requirements, used on farms that needed their help to carry out various works that the farmer didn't have the necessary machinery for, all to help with the production of food and the war effort, the buildings were mainly workshops.

On the right hand side opposite the War-ag, was Mr. Stanley Brawn's Builders yard.

One of my school friends, Jeff Maile lived here with his parents. His Father was brother to Mr. Maurice Maile of Great Stukeley.

Next on the left was the bicycle shop owned by Mr. Harold Brattle, who was a very well known character. His shop was on the corner of Great Northern Street, and to the rear of the shop was a gateway leading on to Spring Common and one time Golf Course. Also on the left was the Coach & Horses public house, and more important to us youngsters, was Mr. Wrigley's sweet shop. (later to become Robinsons) Where on Saturdays whilst shopping with Mother, we would spend our sweet allowance I think it was a shilling at that time, not forgetting our ration coupons.

A little further on was Mr. Jim Jacobs boot and shoe repairs, he also looked after the Huntingdon Town Football Clubs balls and I believe the players boots. Opposite to him was another shop owned by Mr. 'Alfie' Irons. Next on the left was a public house called The White Horse, no longer in existence, then 'The Dolls House' this was where Fenland Potteries were, they made a range of mugs and other items.

Then came 'Toby's Trunk.' Up to this point the road was 'Ermine Street' but it changed here to The High Street. We turned off here to the left for the school. At this point, in the middle of Toby's Trunk, was a large rectangular hole, about twelve feet long by six feet wide. This was let into a water course that flowed under ground from Chivers vegetable processing plant. Chivers covered a large area of ground which is now an industrial site occupied by several companies. This water was and still is under the road past the new police station, under what is now the ring road.

In this opening was a weir with a grating and barriers to collect any rubbish that may have entered at the source. This carries on under ground until it reaches Ambury Road where it is an open brook, and continued open virtually to the river. It was only in culverts to pass under Grammar School Walk, Saint Germain Street and Hartford Road.

We could always tell which vegetables were being processed by the colour of the water, green for peas and red for beetroot. The open section passed the school and was swept once a week by Chivers. The whole of this waterway was built with Staffordshire Blue Engineering Bricks. On the right hand side of this road was the Territorial Army building and, after this point, it was all boarding, belonging to properties with access from Ambury Road.

Most of the ground on the left, after the foot path to Spring Common, was taken over by the American Red Cross and the P.X. these buildings ran right up to Ambury Road. At this point the road became a Dead End with access to Ambury Road via a gate for pedestrians and cyclists; I think some of the buildings were used for nursing.

After the war some of the buildings closest to the school were taken over by the education department. Being used for the art room, (Miss Snitch), Woodwork (Mr. Woodcock) Domestic science I think firstly by Mrs. Woodcock and later by Miss Hamilton.

The playing field opposite our school was for the 'Old Grammar School' which was on the far side of the field. During the war this school was occupied by The Hibury High School for Girls. It was only pulled down in later years to make way for the Anglia Waters new offices. The accommodation for the girls was on the High Street, which is now Iceland, prior to Iceland it was The Eastern Electricity Board, and before that, immediately after the war it was Millers of Cambridge music shop.

Opposite the school was a foot bridge over the brook onto the playing field, at the far side was a wooden building which was the woodworking class room. When I first went to the school Mr. Everett was the woodwork teacher, I remember him as an elderly Gentleman? He was a grumpy old man who wouldn't hesitate at throwing a piece of wood at you if he thought you were not paying attention, or not getting on with your work. Soon after I started at the school the woodwork class was moved to a brick building that was on the side of Grammar School Walk, opposite what is now a Pizza House, next to the county records office. Our school garden was on Grammar School Walk where the flats are now, these were originally built for the water board offices, next to the garden was the Huntingdon Bowls Club green.

During this time there were two other schools in Huntingdon, one was The Common School, so named because it was situated facing Mill Common, access to this school was from Walden road that is now part of the ring road. The building is still there I think it is used by the W.I. and possibly by others.

The other school was The Grammar School situated along the Brampton Road opposite Hinchingbrook Park. I think there were no more than about three hundred pupils there, but because of its status there was a policeman on duty outside the gates mornings and afternoons. Now it has moved across the road into Hinchingbrook house, plus extra new buildings and is a comprehensive school with about 1,500 to 2,000 pupils.

Great Stukeley Hall and Park

Great Stukeley Park was created by the Torkington family at the time of the parliamentary enclosure of 1816, taking in part of Moorfield and parcels of land possessed by St John's and Trinity Colleges in Cambridge. The Torkingtons also closed the way between Owls End and Green End. The flower beds shown were photographed in the late 1870s

A picture of The Hall grounds as date shown. This looked out from the terrace and into the park towards Green End. You can see the boundary (ha-ha!) showing between the trees

At Stukeley Hall in the 1870s the Tillards gave employment to these 18 people photographed outside the coach house. The coach house has been given a new lease of life as a private residence.

These two pictures were reproduced by kind permission of Mr David Cozens from his Huntingdon a Pictorial History

125

I haven't been in Great Stukeley Park for about fifty years, so my memories may be a bit blurred.

In my early years as I recall the main drive from the lodge to the Hall was in regular use.

We sometimes would see a motor car in the drive, with Mrs. Fenwick (Senior) inside. We would refer to her as Lady Fenwick. I learned that she was related to the Manchester Family, The Dukes of Manchester were great land owners in the surrounding area, I know of some of their properties, most of Grafham Village and the farms, and most of the land from there into and beyond Kimbolton.

I don't actually remember speaking to her, but it is likely that she had spoken to all the children in Great Stukeley, when attending functions like the village fete which were sometimes held in the Hall grounds. On one of these occasions I was entered along with Brenda Clark, as 'The Bisto Kids,' in the fancy dress competition, it rained so much that the judging had to be cancelled and every one had to take shelter in one of the buildings near the stables. As there couldn't be any prize giving, all entrants received one shilling. It was well known in the village, that Lady Fenwick offered a piece of ground adjacent to the W.I. hall for the erection of a play area with swings, slide and other equipment. Maybe she was going to finance it herself. But hearsay has it that the offer was withdrawn, because of some unsavoury remarks from one of the parish councillors.

The drive to the hall was sunk to a lower level than the surrounding area, with an avenue of large trees, there were elms, oak and I think some beech. The rest of the park seems to have been altered at various times, or added to. Some of the trees were very old and not planted in any order, but there were signs that at some time other parts had been planned. There was an arrangement of young chestnuts in rows, some pink and others white. There was a narrow band of trees on three sides of the park, that we called the spinney. Starting from the Lodge it runs up the hill following the main road to Green End, then turns and continues parallel to it. In the top corner, near to the rear of the blacksmiths shop, was our cricket pitch, by kind permission of Mr. Fenwick. In the spinney just adjacent to the cricket pitch, where there was a dogleg in the tree line, there was a very large horse chestnut tree in the corner, this is where we gathered our Conkers.

A little further along was the hand gate that we used from the back of our house to cross the park to school, this path crossed over the drive just behind the Lodge, and emerged on the other side onto the main road. In the tree line was a well, we could never understand the reason for this, as there was no building any where near to it We didn't see any water in it, as I recall it had been filled with old barbed wire etc.

There was a five bared gate which led into the park, if you stood at the top of Green End looking towards the Hall, you could see that there had been a roadway from the end of our lane into the park, it was slightly sunken and quite hard because when tractors ran down or across it they left no impression. Adjacent to this gateway there is an old drainage system where there was once an old manor house. There is also a ditch that runs along the line of the old roadway up to the gate, where it disappears underground. This continues on toward the Hall, then at some point it turns and, runs parallel to the drive, under the road at the Lodge and then down 'Waterloo Road' this drain is shown on some of the old maps.

I can remember my father helping some visitors to find the whereabouts of this drain, Father had to do a little digging at the entrance and at the culvert at the other end, I can't remember the actual details, but my Father said that some chemical or dye was used to test the flow. I know it was working at our end, as we use to see it every time we were that way on our travels. It was only about four hundred yards from our house, and the open part of it started alongside our old orchard about forty yards from our back door. There were some large beech trees in this part of the spinney; I wonder if one can still see where we carved our names in the bark? One such tree was just outside the line of the spinney, it had been damaged at some time, possibly by lightning, or a break in its early years. It had rotted away inside the trunk, and then somehow healed itself, leaving a large hole that I could stand upright in when I was about nine or ten, a good hiding place!

The spinney continues on, until it reaches another large gate between the park and the large grass field that ran from behind our old house right down to Grange Farm. Looking across the park there is another large gate exactly opposite. The park here is only about two hundred yards wide, the gate opens onto a roadway running along another arable field, where the Hall is skirted by a large boundary wall about ten feet high, continuing on the same line of sight there is another large gate, shutting off the field, then a short run of about forty yards or so to, yes another large gate, opening onto Owl End. That's four gates all in line.

A little past the first gate, the spinney turns at right angles to the left. In this corner was a small pond, half in the park and half in the spinney. There used to be a pump in the pond for pumping water into a cattle trough. One of my earliest memories, was toddling along holding hands with an old gentleman, across the field to pump the water up.

He was 'Grand dad Green.' He lived in the old railway carriage before Mr. Jacobs. No relation to the other Greens. After about two hundred yards the spinney turns left again. In this corner is the new orchard, bringing us back to the second gate. This is where the wall starts. Just outside the wall a small dog cemetery with little grave stones, I wonder if any one else remembers? I remember Mr. Fenwick having a small terrier with him most of the time. These were Border Terriers.

I recall a pair of beautiful oak trees, we used to call them the twin oaks, they were pretty well identical only about three or four yards apart. One could almost guarantee that there would be some really large mushrooms growing under them.

There were several trees and plantations within the hall grounds, but this was out of bounds to us, so I can't describe the layout. George and I used to be in the park quite a lot. We were always told to keep well away from the Hall. 'People don't you gawping at them,' Mother would say. There is another small pond in the park, this is close to the Lodge. We could never understand why it was there. It was completely fenced in and had bushes growing all round, so it wasn't for cattle to drink from. Several trees were cut down in the park during my younger years. We could see the stumps that were left. One in particular I remember, as I saw it being cut down, I was about twelve years old then, it was a large elm tree just to the right of the footpath, and about twenty yards inside the park. This was the first time I saw a double headed axe, the man using it used to turn it over as he swung it back, so that both edges were used alternately.

On the far side from us there were two rings of small thorn hedges about twelve or fourteen yards across with fir trees planted inside. We could never find out what these were for, we had asked several people about them, even my Father didn't know what they were for, so I suppose that they were there as a feature, but there isn't any thing like it anywhere else in the park.

Continuing along the boundary in the other direction from the Lodge up to Owl End, there are no trees along this part, just a hedge, which continues up to the village hall where it turns right and follows the line of Owl End continuing with a hedge until it reaches a wide iron gate then a high boarded fence, with trees on the inside until it reaches the walled garden, not visible from the road. At the end of the war the large walled garden was turned over to market gardening. Some of the produce was sold in Huntingdon, I recall seeing Mr. Fenwick unloading vegetables at 'Alfie Iron's' Shop I don't know if all the produce was sold locally. I expect that Mr. Fenwick's enterprise was similar to that of Mr. Charlie Deller Snr. I think he turned to market gardening for financial reasons, to help with the running of the Hall.

After the walled garden the boundary continues on to the rear entrance to the hall. Then we come to the wall coming from the other direction which I mentioned earlier, and that completes the boundary as I remember it.

Just short of the rear entrance, outside the wall, was the old gardeners house, I don't remember it as being habitable but it was still complete and was being used for storage, and as the potting shed. We often use to see Mr. Cole working there when we were on our travels. It has gone now and a new house is in its place.

I can't say much about the Hall, as the only times we had any reason to be in the grounds was for garden fetes, except the time we got caught on the swing, so I have no recollection of any of the features. From the front, or east side it looked like a very nice place. There was a wide flight of steps leading down to the lawn from the terrace running down to an iron railing fence, and a 'Ha Ha', making it very open from this side.

Clubs and Groups

During the years after the war I joined a variety of clubs and organizations. George had gone back home to London as soon as the war ended. He had just completed his education at the age of fourteen. I was eleven then and still had a lot of schooling to do.

I had joined one of these prior to George leaving, the Cubs. George was too old, as Cub membership had to end at eleven years old. I myself only had about a year in the Cubs. The meetings were held in an old house in Newton's Court in Huntingdon. Although this area of town has mainly been re-developed the old house is still there, and it is classified as a 'Listed Building.' At one time it had been a Public House and there is an old name plate on the wall. After the Cubs I joined the Houghton Scout Troupe along with George Gough, one of my pals from Great Stukeley. We use to cycle there once a week, joining up with two boys from Hartford, Ray Smith and his younger brother. I stayed in the Scouts for about two years, but with so much going on at that time I lost interest and left.

I joined the Meccano Club. My parents having bought me a No.1 Set, which was the smallest set for beginners, and all they could afford at the time. The club meetings were held at Saint Johns Hall, one time Saint Johns Church. We had to take in any models we had built for appraisal. These were assessed on the size and type of sets that you owned at the time. The head of the club was a Mr. John Deves, who was the manager of the B.C.&.H. Electric Company, (Beds, Cambs, & Hunts). Later to become Eastern Electric Company, whose head quarters were in George Street.

Later on I was fortunate enough to obtain a No. 2 set, with extras, from a boy at school whose family were emigrating to Australia.

At the club we sometimes had visitors who would give lectures on various subjects. One I remember in particular gave a talk on nature, and bird life, he made deliberate mistakes in his talk, and the idea was to spot these and write them down, the boy with the most correct answers would win a prize. And on this occasion it was me. My prize was a Guillemots Egg, which I still have. This would be illegal now, but not sixty years ago.

Another club I joined was 'The Bunny Club' this was organized by The Hunts Post. The emblem was a white enamel rabbit on a bronze badge, I still have mine, and it was passed onto me by Louise Clark, a neighbour of ours. There was a news letter every week in the 'Hunts Post' written by 'Uncle Bunny.' The club was a charity really for children in hospital. We collected 'Bun Pennies' these were Queen Victorian pennies showing the Queen without a head dress, thus being able to see the 'Bun' at the back of her head.

I was a little disappointed once. Having collected the pennies for some time, I proudly went to the 'Hunts Post' office clutching my little bag of coins and into the 'Bunny Office' only to find that 'Uncle Bunny' was really an 'Aunty Bunny.' Yes Uncle Bunny was really a lady.

At fourteen I joined the youth club in Huntingdon. The club was in some old war time 'Nissen' huts which were situated between Castle Hills and the now funeral parlour of Messrs Peacock. This particular building was the head quarters of the R.A.F's. Pathfinder Group and was Bomb Proof. Having seen the structure in recent times when builders have tried to make alterations to the walls, I can believe this to be so. That is why the government building got the name Pathfinder House. Certainly not bomb proof, becoming unsafe after only thirty years. The leader when I joined was Pete Reynolds, soon to be taken over by Mr. Walsh. Pete was a younger man, more sporty and lively, Mr. Walsh was a more mature person. He was in local government, and a good leader. His door was always open if you needed advice or help in any way. He was very calm and pleasant and showed an interest in every thing that was going on.

There was a small canteen where you could have a cup of tea or soft drink and other light refreshments. On the games side we had a ¼ size snooker table, table tennis and many activities. Dancing was one of these and one of my few regrets in life is that I didn't learn to dance properly.

One of the smaller rooms in the club had easy chairs and tables, where we could just sit and read or have a conversation amongst our selves. Quite often there would be an organized discussion on various subjects, and sometimes Mr. Walsh would sit in on these. I remember one of these talks touched on the subject of sex, and we had to get written permission from our parents to join in with this. This was for the younger members.

I was fourteen at that time, and the club was open for persons up the age of twenty one.

One sporting opportunity was to join the rowing club. The youth club, and a few of us participated in this. We had training sessions with the senior members of the rowing club, who were keen to have us there, thinking of the future no doubt to build up a young team so as to carry on when some of the older members dropped out. Unfortunately only two of us stuck to it. That was Bill James from Godmanchester and me. With the lack of support that ended.

My main interest in the club was the boxing department. We had at a very good team, and a good trainer in Bert Twigden, who had been a good boxer in his younger years.

He had very good hands, and dealt with most problems arriving from any injuries we managed to collect. He used to treat anyone for sprains and strains, unofficially of course. Our team leader was Don (J.J.) Brading, a brilliant boxer and very skilful, his brother Bob was also in our team, both came from Godmanchester. Then there were the four Williams brothers from Little Stukeley, John Tack from Huntingdon, who had a left hand like a rapier, that many a professional would have been proud of. On one occasion we were boxing at Ramsey in the County Championships John was drawn against the favourite for the championship, at his weight. Before the proceedings started the father of John's opponent came into the dressing room and suggested to Burt that his boy would be

> ## LIMELIGHT
>
> A KNOCK-OUT, and grand display by tw[o] schoolboy boxers were fea[-]tures of a boxing show stage[d] by Ramsey Youth Club o[n] Friday at the Old Cinema.
> Contestants came from S[t] Neots, Huntingdon, Woodsto[n] and Ramsey youth clubs. I[n] the schoolboy contest Cole, o[f] Ramsey, gained the verdic[t] after an exciting and gam[e] tussle with Harlock.
> Tack (Huntingdon), prove[d] an aggresive and hard-hit[-]ting fighter and knocked ou[t] Bent, of Ramsey.
> One of the best fights wa[s] that between Lovell (Hunt[-]ingdon) and Burridge (St Neots), the former winning on points.
> Bolton (St. Neots) rathe[r]

much too good for John, and that he ought not to be allowed to box.

Bert replied that he thought that his boy would be O.K. At this the other man shrugged his shoulders and walked off. In the first round not much happened, the other lad looked a bit classy, up in his toes and prancing about a bit, a bit of a show off really. Early in the second round John had had enough of this 'messing around' having made an opening in the other lads defence, he dropped his left shoulder and brought over the sweetest left hook you could wish for, dropping his opponent to the canvas, being unable to raise, he was counted out, a knock out win for John. The other lad was unsteady for some time.

Bert's nephew Ted used to turn up when he was on leave from the army and perform for us. There were a few lads that only stayed for one season, not really suited for the job, but had a go anyway. We had a boy from Brampton, Peter Benson, who used to box at about six and a half stones; I don't think he weighed more than about nine stones when he was a grown man. He was very good, a bit of a Barry Mc Guigan.

When I was sixteen and seventeen I boxed at eleven and a half stones, so a big lad, and did manage to win the area championship twice. I received a small silver cup, about the size of an egg cup, nowadays it would possibly be the size of the F.A. Cup. But in 1950 - 51 things were in short supply, but I thought just as much of these as any one would to-day, what ever the size.

We once had a competition with R.A.F. Wyton. But I was not allowed to box on this occasion, I was drawn against a senior who was a corporal P.T. instructor aged about twenty six. I was classed as a junior at sixteen but although being the right weight the bout was called off, much to my disappointment, I suppose I would have been given a good pasting, so no doubt it was for the best. This was a problem for me being at that weight as a junior, it was difficult to find opponents in the same class, I always thought that I was 'good at the game,' having been taught the art by my Father who was an experienced boxer himself. There was always a set of gloves in our house, Father used to spar with me in the back yard at home, and any one else who wanted a go.

At about the same time here was another club formed in Huntingdon, The Cromwell Athletic Club, which I joined with one or two others who were keen to partake in all sports. I was advised to take up the Javelin and Shot Put because of my stature, I was never very fast over the ground, although the Javelin did require a run, but having broad shoulders and a good arm this seemed to compensate for the short run up. The training went quite well and I was getting fairly good at both disciplines, as there were no competitions with other clubs the competition came from within the club itself. Unfortunately it all became a bit Cliquey and Snobbish I am afraid the attitude was that if one came from The Council School you were inferior to the people that came from The Grammar School.

School sports were improving though. We had a football and a cricket team which I played for. We had school sports days, with competitions between the four 'houses.' I wasn't very fast, I wasn't overweight then but always heavy for my age, but when playing foot ball I took a bit of stopping. I didn't get knocked off the ball very often.

We had a professional football coach come to the school, for a one day visit. He was Frank Sou, or Soo, he had Oriental looking features, and came from The Arsenal.

We had inter-school sports where we had competitions with other schools within the county. These were mainly for track events, as we were not geared up for the field events like shot, javelin or discus. It was an opportunity to select the best in the county to compete in the all England schools competition.

A few from our school were quite good. There was one in particular was Lawrence Burton from Great Stukeley, he could run at almost any distance and was selected to compete for the county.

This competition was held at Port Sunlight, but sadly he didn't do very well. He was running in school plimsolls against boys running in Spikes and with top class coaching. But at least he had the honour of representing his county.

At the end of the war village sport began to get off the ground. We had a combined Great. and Little Stukeley cricket team, and in 1946 we won the Cranfield League much to the delight to both villages. We played Yelling in the final which was held at the Offord's Cricket Ground. This was a bit of a nail biter, Yelling batted first and made a pretty good score. This was a rather rough pitch, and we lost two early wickets.

Father batted at No. 4. As he went into bat the captain, Jim Pinner, said to him, 'Keep your end up Art. We have to play this one out, I don't think we can win here.' He did just that, batting for almost an hour, a long time in a village game, seeing a steady fall of wickets for very few runs. When the last man, Jack Pinner, came there were about ten minutes left to play, Father told to him just take a single, and let me take the bowling, Jack was not the best bat in the team. Fortunately they managed that single and father took the rest of the bowling and a single of the last ball of each over, and they batted out for a draw much to the delight to the rest of the team and supporters. Father was the hero of the day then, but he was always my hero.

The return match was held at Buckden where Yelling batted first again scoring 65 runs,

Jim Pinner hit the winning run at 66, I think we won by about four wickets.

There was much celebrating done at the Three Horseshoes that night.

Our pitch was used by permission of Mr. Fenwick of Great Stukeley Hall, he was the club president. There was some disappointment that George Gifford of Grange Farm didn't take an interest in the club. He was a first class cricketer, playing for Huntingdon for several years, and was a keen supporter and benefactor of that club for some time after his playing days were over. I think there is still a trophy in his name now.

It was rumoured that when he was a young man, he could have played for Northamptonshire as a full time player. But his Father, Mr. Josh. Gifford told George it was either farming or cricket and that he couldn't do both, and that if he chose cricket he would cut him out of the farm.

The cricket team carried on for a number of years, I played when I was sixteen and seventeen. We also had a football team at about the same time, but we didn't do as well in this as we did at cricket. People use to say that the Stukeley team was made up of young boys and old men, which was quite true, and we would get beaten by as many as ten goals, but we enjoyed playing

I was a regular in the football team when I was sixteen, along with one or two more youngsters. People like my Father, Charlie Deller, Wally Waldock, Bob Stukins and Ted Porter all played at the time. (The old men) Ted Porter was the only man I can remember turning up with highly polished football boots; they had a better shine on than some people's Sunday shoes. We played then, as now, in the field next to the Three Horseshoes.

There was a big depression in the corner, Ted Porter played on the left wing, and this dip was known as 'Porters Grave.' He could put over a centre from here landing at the feet of the center forward nearly every time.

We used to practice whenever we could; we boys would be there almost every evening after getting home from school. One evening, Jimmy Elsome called in for a kick about straight from work. We took turns at being in goal. When it was Jimmies turn, whilst still wearing his boiler suit, he dived across the goal to make a save, and on making contact with the ground the friction set fire to a box of 'Swan' matches in his pocket, causing bit of a panic for a minute or two. No real damage was done but the goalmouth was littered with burnt out matches for some time.

I played football, cricket also boxed until I was conscripted into the army at eighteen, to do my National Service. My sporting activities then came to an end.

My Mothers younger sister, Marjory was married to Ron Brown, who came from Broughton. Uncle Ron was a well known sports man, cricket being his favourite game, but he was also a good footballer. He played football for Brampton around about the same time as my Father, Father having stopped playing when I was born in 1934. Ron Brown being a bit younger than Father carried on playing for Brampton for a few more years.

In 1949 whilst playing cricket for Huntingdon, (he was probably the best wicket keeper for miles around.)

He was struck on the heart by a fast rising ball. He was unsighted as the ball passed the batsman, because he always stood up close, even to the fasted bowlers. After being struck he rubbed his chest and indicated to the other players that he was O.K. After taking the next over at the other end he then faced the fast bowling again. He took another blow in the same place, and collapsed to the ground. All efforts to revive him failed and he died on the field. The doctor told my Aunt Marge that the first blow would have been fatal, as it had burst a valve in his heart. When he died he not only left my aunt, but also a baby daughter, (my cousin Marian) who was just over one year old.

Marge and Ron were married just after the war. I believe they were engaged before he was called up. He served in North Africa and was taken prisoner, and served four years in a German P.O.W. camp. Uncle Ron worked for a building company in Somersham, and had to have time off from work to play mid week games, unpaid I believe.

He lost his life doing something he loved, but at the age of just thirty, a great tragedy.

Working in My School Years

From the age of twelve we were allowed to work on the farm to help with the harvest.

One had to register with the youth employment department, and was issued with a 'Yellow card.' I did this for the next three years. If you had worked full time through the summer holidays, (called the harvest holidays) and the farmer needed you, you were allowed extra time off to help finish off the grain harvest and carry on with the potato lifting. You would probably have six or eight weeks of sunshine, all through the harvest and even into September when we were getting the potatoes up, the sun used to come through the mist at about ten-o-clock, and become quite warm. What ever happened to our summers? Maybe we only remember the good ones.

My first week at work was for Mr. Gifford at Grange Farm. I had to start work at the same time as the men, seven -o-clock and work until seven or eight in the evening.

When I went to draw my wages on Friday, I received the large sum of twelve shillings and sixpence. When I was paid, I told Mr. Gifford that I wouldn't be coming back again, 'Why Why What What?' he asked in his peculiar way of speaking. I replied that I was going to work for Mr. Juggins and he was going to pay me one pound per week for less hours. 'Good, good, good!' was his reaction. I don't think he listened to what any one said most of the time.

There was a story about him not paying attention to what people were saying, when at St. Ives market one day. He asked a farmers young son, 'How's Father How's Father?' The young mans reply was. 'I am sorry to say Mr. George, we lost him last week.' 'Good good!' he said and walked away.

I settled down at Mr. Juggins' working with Brian and Doug Sewell, and the rest of his men, working with the horses and driving the tractors. There were four work horses, plus Mr. Juggins' riding horse. The two main horses were both mares, a gray called Blossom and a black one called Bonny, then there was a smaller horse, his name was Punch. He always had a smaller or lighter load than the two big mares

The forth one called Captain was not fully broken and he was only used for muck carting he would stand whilst his cart was being loaded, as soon as he was moved he wanted to gallop. Brian Sewell was the only one that could handle him, and he had to run with him all the time. This horse only worked up to about twelve o'clock. But Brian, who had been running all morning, still had to work the rest of the day.

Although I could drive the tractors well enough, I was not able to work the binder, which required a lot of skill especially when turning in on the corners. It was so easy to get it wrong and run onto the standing crop and spoil a lot of grain. But I was allowed to do this in my third season.

I was able to do most things on the farm, with a little guidance, and was well thought of by Mr. Juggins. The barley crop was slightly different, inasmuch it was not always put up into stooks, but what was called rowed in, this was a process of making one row out of five, or sometimes four depending on the density of the crop, the idea was for two men to move the two outside rows into the middle fifth and make a continues row, this made it easier when loading it onto the carts.

There were three tractors on Mr. Juggins' farm, two John Deere's and a very old 'Farmall,' this was made by the International Harvester Co. One John Deere was the same model as Mr. Gifford's, which I described earlier; the other one was a normal four wheel type. The small model was used for all general farm work and all through the harvest. As soon as a harvest field was free the larger one was taken off corn carting and used for ploughing, and was driven by Douglas Sewell. Sometimes the ploughing would be going on in the same field when the corn was being carted off.

The old Farmall was used solely for pea cutting and had a cutter fitted to it permanently, and was brought out of retirement for one week each year; The peas that Mr. Juggins grew were harvested in a ripened, not green, state and I suppose were classed as 'Dried Peas.' This old machine was driven by Mr. Jim Haynes. One day one of the large rear wheels came off, and left poor Jim sitting at a precarious angle, still holding onto the steering wheel for support.

Two of Mr. Juggins' fields were next to the railway where the track was on the same level as the field before going into the cutting. When the harvest was ready a team of men from the railway company used to come and mow the crop for about ten yards into the field, this was done with scythes and carried out to prevent any possibility of the field being set on fire with sparks from the engines, or cinders from the fireboxes.

This could easily have happened as you could see where there had been fires along the railway embankment. The grass etc. would have been tinder dry, so would have only needed one spark to start such a fire. Not as much of that risk now with our wetter summers! - And no steam engines.

I worked for Mr. Juggins for three full harvests, at the ages of Twelve, Thirteen and Fourteen. The wages went up a little each year. This enabled me to help with my keep. Mother didn't take any money from me, but I was able to buy some of my requirements myself.

At the end of my second harvest I had saved enough money to buy my own new bicycle.

It was a Robin Hood, this was a model made by the Raleigh Co. It was just a plain sports model, no gears. It cost £14.00 from Curry's. But I was as proud of this as anyone buying a Harley Davidson.

At the end of each harvest I used to take the two mares to have new shoes fitted, this meant riding one, side saddle, and leading the other into Huntingdon to the Blacksmiths, Mr. Harry Standen,

Whose yard was situated in Princess Street, behind where the old fire station used to be, at the back of Woolworth's, now Sports & Fashions, I wouldn't fancy the journey today. But it was quite safe then, only one motor car about every five minutes.

A 'Farmall' tractor made by the International Harvester Co. USA. This is the type we had on Mr Juggins' farm, the one that Jim Hayes was driving when the wheel came off!

Top: *John Deer Model 'H' tractor as used at Grange Farm also on Mr Juggins' farm*

Bottom: *Early model 'Fordson' tractor as used at Grange Farm*

143

A 'Binder' that cut the standing crop, tied it into bundles and dropped in rows ready to be picked up and carted off.

A John Deere model 'B' Mr Juggins' second tractor, his other one was a model 'H' like the one at Grange farm

Later model of the 'Standard' Fordson tractor

Punch, the smaller horse didn't have shoes, neither did Captain. I also used to take Mr. Juggins' riding horse in for shoeing, but not on the same day. I used to have the bridal on but not the saddle, I was able to sit astride him, but without the saddle I could only walk him, no doubt this was done for my safety.

Mentioning Woolworth's reminds me of my trips into town with Mother. Just inside the door on the right hand side was an ice cream counter. There was only one type of ice cream, and a few triangular iced lollies, the ice creams were round, flat on top and bottom and had a thin cardboard ring round them which would be removed before putting them into a cone, we thought this was heaven after all the war time restrictions. Sports & fashions still have the same old 'Woollies' door.

Mr. Sewell senior, was the shepherd for Mr. Juggins and when he retired Brian took over this job. He became 'famous' and had his picture on the front page of the Hunts Post. He was the first local shepherd to have a ewe give birth to healthy triplets.

Mr. Juggins also had three Irish men come to help with the harvest, they slept in the barn, I think Mrs. Juggins gave them palliasses for their beds, and fed them. They only stayed for a short period when the most work was being carried out, I think they used to travel from farm to farm.

Being classed as a full time worker qualified me for extra rations. This was a national concession for agricultural workers, due to very hard work and long hours. These rations were issued every Friday along with the wages. Mrs. Juggins would set them out in a row of boxes, and as you left with your money you picked up your box.

There was butter, cheese, sugar and one or two more items that I can't recall, but every one appreciated the extras.

On one occasion when trying to get a field cleared before dark we had taken both tractors down to the field, as the horses were not worked after tea, to try and get all the remaining crop onto the two trailers. This we managed, but only just. I don't think there had ever been two larger loads on two wheeled trailers before. Mr. Juggins only had the smaller type of trailer, unlike Mr. Gifford who had some really large ones, that had been articulated lorries originally, and would have cleared our field with only one of these.

We managed it. I brought the last cart home with the four wheeled John Deere. By this time it was quite dark, gone nine-o-clock. It was at the end of August, and the exhaust manifold showed red hot in the dark. This wasn't a problem though as you could always see this in the dark on all tractors. My Father came looking for me; he had had his supper and was thinking of going to bed. He had a few words with Roger about me being at work so late. Nothing was said in an angry way, just that he didn't want me out working so late. He knew it was my own fault, because I didn't have to go if I didn't want to.

Another amusing thing that happened in the harvest field one day was when Mr. Sewell Sen. ran into the straw stack with the tractor. We were using tractors and horses at the same time. On this occasion when Mr. Sewell brought a horse down the field with an empty cart, it was a tractor that was ready to be taken back to the thrashing machine.

Mr. Sewell didn't like driving the tractors, but he took this one anyway, upon drawing up along side the thrashing machine, instead of operating the clutch to stop the tractor, he said Whoa! Whoa! as though to stop a horse, of cause the tractor didn't obey the command and ran into the straw stack. By this time Mr. Sewell remembered he was driving a tractor and not a horse, and managed to stop it before it buried itself in the stack. All three of my harvest seasons with Mr. Juggins were enjoyable, and a happy time, hard work sometimes, but I was never made to do anything that I didn't want to.

On Saturdays, during school time, I used to help around the farm, cleaning out the hen house, and collecting Mrs. Juggins' eggs, they were just for the house.. I used to mix the food for the calves. There were always a few of these as Mr. Juggins always had two or three milking cows. Jim Haynes looked after these. Working horses can't live on grass alone, so there was their food to prepare which I sometimes helped Ted Cox with. They had oats, chaff and cut up mangoldes. The calves had a similar mix, but they didn't have oats but they had 'cow cake.' This came in slabs about an inch thick and two feet square, which was put through a 'cake breaker' that broke the slabs into little pieces about an inch square. All the ingredients were mixed together on the floor of the feed store, then molasses (black treacle) was poured into the mix and stirred in. (But not for the horses.) This came in a forty gallon barrel, and had a tap fitted I used to draw off a measured amount into a large jug to add to the mix, 'accidentally on purpose' getting some on my fingers, the only way to clean your fingers was to lick it off. Lovely, I learned this trick from Mr. Haynes, who also told me to take some home in a jam jar for Mother to make a treacle cake, which I did.

When the animals were fed with this mixture all the feeding troughs and other vessels were licked clean, almost to a shine, so it must have been good.

Farmers still used this molasses to make silage until quite recently, when I think it became too expensive.

All through the harvests, and potato lifting, Mr. Jim Haynes's wife Rose worked on the farm, she worked alongside the men and could do all the things the men could do, she even drove the tractors when we were 'carting off.'

George Gough, Mrs. Haynes's nephew Harry (her son), me and one or two others, used to play cricket outside her house, taking turns at batting and bowling.

She often joined in when she wasn't too busy, and she could bowl over arm!

She was a well built lady and could bowl a decent ball, some times better than us boys.

I could whistle a good tune then, but we weren't allowed to whistle at school, I couldn't read music, and still can't, but have a good ear for music of all kinds. Mrs. Haynes realized this and wanted to enter me for 'The Carol Levis' Discovery program on the radio.

This was a talent show where you could write in to enter, or have someone enter you.

If selected on the information given you were invited to go to London for an audition. She also wanted to enter me for auditions for 'Just William' another radio program for children, but neither of these materialized. Just think, I could have been 'A Star.'

Another person in the village wanted to give me a helping hand at one of my other talents, he was Mr. Denny Sly, a full time professional sports photographer, specializing in boxing. He wanted my parents to let him take me to London and introduce me to the Jack Solomans' gymnasium and club, from where all the boxing from the south of England was run. Jack Solomons was one of the biggest boxing promoters in the country.

Any boy from any club who showed potential as a boxer was welcome to have a trial at 'Jack Solomon's.' If any one showed any real chance of making the grade he would be taken under the wing of the organization, and brought along at the right pace.

My parents declined the offer, thanking Mr. Sly for his kindness but it would have meant me staying away from home for a time, even for the initial trials. On reflection I don't think that I would have made the grade, I didn't have the experience that all the London club boys would have had. I would have been in good company, 'Our Enery,' Henry Cooper was a Jack Soloman's boy; the same age as me.

***

When the Clark family lived next door to us their son Arthur didn't have a regular job, but set himself up as a market trader. He dealt in poultry, eggs, rabbits and that sort of thing. He had a very old motor, it was about a nineteen twenty model, a 'Bull Nosed' Morris Cowley that had been made into a truck. This was the model that had a big brass radiator, and cast iron 'Artillery' wheels. It would be worth a fortune today.

When I was on holiday from school I used to spend quite a lot of time with him. He used to take me to the markets. St. Ives, St. Neots, Thrapston, Royston and sometimes further afield. He used to let me drive his old motor on the main road, when I was fourteen. On one of our return trips from London, I drove it all the way from Royston to home.

The London trips usually involved taking eggs to some hotels. Hens eggs were still on ration, so most of them were turkey and goose eggs bought in the local markets and from farmers. There would also be poultry for the table. The hotels we went to were always down a back street. I suppose it was all a bit 'Hush! Hush' a little bit of black market. We went to several of these places, and the truck was always well loaded when we left home, so no doubt it was a good income for Arthur. He was a well known character, and a little bit shady. Every one at the markets knew him. He didn't have a game license, but he sometimes had pheasants in his truck. When he sold these in the market he gave a local butchers name as the vendor, saying that he was selling them for him. Not true, as most people knew, but nothing was ever done about it. I suppose at that time many were 'at it.'

I remember one occasion in particular, we were at Royston market and Arthur asked me to hang a brace of pheasants on the hooks in the sale room for game. On doing so the auctioneers assistant asked whose they were I replied as instructed with the butcher's name. 'Oh' he said, 'That B****y Clarkie' s here is he.'

Like I say, a well known character. With his truck being classed as a commercial vehicle he could use red petrol in it, but the customs people were very strict on the use of these motors. I had seen him put a crate of hens in the back when he went courting, just to be on the safe side. One Sunday he even had a dead goat in it. Goats were eaten regularly then. During the same years that I worked on the farm, I also earned some pocket money from Arthur, doing a lot of poultry plucking for him.

His Father had a large shed at the bottom of the garden. I used to spend hours at a time plucking in that shed. The sort of plucking required was called rough plucked. After a short time I was able to kill the birds as well. Someone had to do it, and after the first few it didn't bother me, I used to dispatch the hens and the cockerels, but not ducks or geese, Arthur used to do these.

Hens and cockerels were easy to pluck, but ducks and especially geese were difficult, they virtually had to be plucked twice, feathers off the first time over, then the down taken off separately. There was even a market for the feathers.

Arthur paid me nine pence for hens and cockerels, a shilling for ducks and half a crown for geese. I once plucked twelve hens in one night, about three hours.

'Odds And Ends'

When I was about eight I used to spend quite a bit of time at Mrs. Thackray's house with their eldest son John, who was younger than me.

I used to go to his birthday parties and at other times to play. This carried on for a few years although not on a regular basis. Then in 1945 just as the war was ending, Mr. & Mrs. Thackray decided that as part of the celebrations they would have a big Guy Faulkes party for the children of Green End. This meant getting organized, to collect as much material for the Bonfire as we could find. There were a few of us boys, Harry Haynes, Brian Smith Ron Jacobs, his brother Albert had already left school and was working for Mr. Thackray in the building trade. Then there was George and me. We had a few weeks notice to collect quite a large amount of wood, old things that people had thrown out for us, and any rubbish that would burn. The fire was not built straight away, so the material was stored in one of Mr. Thackray's barns, to keep it tidy and dry. We built the fire two days before the 5th of November then on the actual morning Mr. Thackray's lorry driver brought a lorry load of scrap timber and wood shavings from the works in Huntingdon and this was added to the fire. It was quite huge when it was all put together. Someone had made a big 'Guy' and put him on the top.

The fireworks were organized by Mr. Guy Fisher; who was Mrs. Thackray's brother. The Fisher Family had a business in Huntingdon. I believe it was his birthday, hence the name Guy.

He supplied a tea chest full of fireworks, something we had never seen before, not like today's standard, but spectacular enough at the time. There were Rockets, Roman Candles, Catherine Wheels, Golden Rain, Squibs and many others, including 'bangers,' which the boys were allowed to let off. We were given handfuls of them.

This event went on for the next few years, the fireworks getting bigger and better each time. The Catherine Wheels then were the size of dinner plates and the rockets developed into the high flying exploding type. And the Roman Candles were so big they had to be fixed to the fence.

Mothers Hair.

My mother had beautiful long auburn hair that reached right down to her waist in two long plaits. These were turned three times round her ears and then crossed over at the back of her head, I think the style was called 'Ear Muffs,' and Victorian looking. She never wore it loose, although it did look nice when she combed it out, as it was wavy.

One day two of the girls next door, Olive and Louie Clark suggested that she 'ought to get with it' and have it cut and permed in a modern style. After much deliberation and discussion she agreed to have it done. The girls said that they would get all the necessary materials for a home perm and they would do it for her.

As cutting was being carried out Mother cried, the two girls cried, and so did I. Father never said a word, but every one knew how he felt about it. And for a long time afterwards Mother regretted having it cut. I can't recall what happened to her hair. I think she should have kept it, but I don't think she did.

Mother's hair didn't thin with age and she still had a full head of hair when she died at ninety two. Naturally it was white by this time.

The Wicksteed Park Saga.

After the war when things were getting back to normal, trips were organized to various places. For us it was Wicksteed Park.

All the swings, slides, roundabouts, rocking horses, rings and climbing ropes etc. were free. But we paid to go on the train, water chute, boating lake and one or two other things. But entry to the zoo was free.

On these outings some of the women went off to Kettering to look round the shops, while the others looked after the children. Our Mothers enjoyed looking in the larger shops. My mother went off on the first trip to town, she had only been in town for a short while, when someone said to her 'Your boy has fallen into the lake.' Mother rushed back as fast as her legs would carry her, it was only one mile. 'Where is my boy, is he alright?' she cried. 'Of course he is' said Mrs. Haynes, who had dried my clothes. Only my trousers had got wet, and I was playing as though nothing had happened. What the messenger hadn't told Mother was that I had only fallen into the Kiddies Paddle Boat Lake, this was only about fourteen to sixteen inches deep. Mother had visions of people dragging the big lake for me, It took some time for her to get over the panic, and spoiled the rest of her day.

Snowed In

In the winter of 1946 we had a great deal of snow, more than any of us had seen before.

Green End was cut off. The snow had filled the cut between Mr. Molecaster's house on one side, and across to the Blacksmiths Shop and bank on the other.

This blocked the main road, to depth of about eight to ten feet. It took a long time to open up the road again, and for a long time there was only room for one vehicle to pass through. The road into Huntingdon was covered with hard packed snow, so we had to walk to school for some time. It was good fun though, we played snow balls all the way to school and back again.

Once on my way home from school, with Brian Smith, George Gough, and one or two others, we got as far as the cottages adjacent to the bus depot, when Brian Smith's auntie, (who lived in one of the cottages) started a snowball fight with us, it was great fun until, Mr. Shelton from Little Stukeley Post Office passed by with his son Selwyn, and got caught in the cross fire. He got one right in his ear, thrown by me unfortunately.

Mr. Shelton wasn't the most pleasant man and this really upset him. He said he was going for the police, report us all to the school, see all our parents and goodness knows what else. Mrs. Smith drew him to one side and said not to be such a spoil sport. He went off in a huff but nothing was ever heard about it

The snow stayed with us for a long time, although the school didn't close. Some of the children from outlaying villages were unable to attend, due to roads being blocked I think we had a covering of about one foot all over the whole area, and more in places where it had drifted.

Some of us boys had a great time in the Stukeley park. We made big snow balls then rolled them over and over until they were so big we couldn't see over them. We started between the cricket pitch and the hand gate at the rear of our house, when we got them as big as we could, we rolled them down the slope towards the driveway to the hall, they gained speed and size at a great rate, completely out of our control. I think the largest one was about eight feet in diameter when it eventually stopped. We got a bit of a telling off for this because they did take a long time to melt, and were still there a long time after the other snow had gone.

When the snow did eventually melt, it was well into February, there were some quite serious floods. Alconbury suffered the worse in our area.

On arriving at school one day, we assembled in the main hall as usual, only to be told that the school would have to close, due to the boiler house being flooded and there was no heating.

Several instructions were given by Mr. Slater, the head. 'Children that came by bus will wait in the school while arrangements could be made for their departure.'

'Those of you that walked to school should now go straight home, and no loitering in the town, and no fooling around on the way home'

'Those of you that cycled in should do likewise'

Did the Stukeley boys obey? No chance.

We heard that the water was coming over the road at 'Nuns Bridge' by Hinchingbrook. So off we went to have a look. We were stopped in our tracks on our way down to the bridge by a policeman who told us that the road was impassable, but we were allowed to have a look at the water. On the Brampton side of the bridge was an A.A. man measuring the depth of the water, he told every one, (there was quite a gathering by this time), that the water was twenty eight inches deep and rising. Brampton like several other places was cut off, and people unable to get into town for some time.

Developing Stukeley.
In 1945 the building of council houses started in Gt. Stukeley. This first stage was Moorfieldfield Way. There were twelve houses to be built, but they weren't completed until 1948. There was a long lay off in the 46/47 winter, due to bad weather.

From information I gathered from the records office, the development of these houses was proposed in June 1945, and agreed in September 1945. The roads and sewers were started. The road being completed in December and the first footings were dug In March 1946. Normal progress was maintained, i.e. drains, footings, paths and all usual ground work, until that long winter set in. All works ceased then until March 1947.

The first pair were let and occupied on 20th. October 1947.

With the exception of two of these houses, which were let to residents of Little Stukeley, all went to Great Stukeley people.

During the same period temporary housing was developed for council staff and civil servants like police, firemen, and council office staff. These were timber houses and were built in a field next to the old 1919 houses adjacent to the main road. When Mr. Gifford farmed this and the next field they were known as 'The Council Fields.' So I assume that the ground belonged to the council to start with.

There were a few private houses built around this time, in Church End. Others followed later on. Now the village is just about full.

Surprise Visit.

One Saturday afternoon, in 1946 George turned up at Green End on a bicycle, a top of the range sports/ racing bike.

He liked riding out of London, and on this particular day, having ridden as far as Royston, Thought to him self, 'Well I am half way to Stukeley why not carry on.'

So he did, on seeing him at the door, Mother started to panic, 'Do your parents know where you are? Have you run away?' Explaining that he was just out for a ride, Mother calmed down and said how pleased she was to see him.

It was quite late in the afternoon, and mother said, 'You can't ride all that way back to night. What are we going to do?' At this point Father took over in his usual calm way. 'First of all,' he said, 'we must try and let your parents know that you are here with us, and that every thing is O.K.'

Father went up to Mr. Juggins and asked if he could phone the police, to see if they could get the London police to help. Mr. Juggins was well known and had friends in the police force.

Father came back saying, 'Every thing is in order' and 'Mr. Juggins has been very helpful, and George's people have been informed.'

George stayed until Sunday afternoon. About four o'clock Father and I went to the railway station, to see George off, he put his bike in the guards van, which was allowed in those days.

After this first visit it became a fairly regular thing. He arrived on Saturday afternoon and cycled home on Sunday.

One Saturday he gave Mother a bit of a shock. He had arrived in Huntingdon, and remembering that Mother would be on the market, decided to have a look to see if she was there. She was, so George crept up behind her, tapped her on the shoulder, and said, 'What are you buying then,' almost causing Mother to drop her shopping. After a little chastisement she said how pleased she was to see him again, and we all had another pleasant week end.

After George had been back in London about two years, his mother died after a long illness. Soon after that he came back to us on a permanent basis, back where he wanted to be, Father got him a job on the farm, and he stayed there until he was called up for national service. He married a Stukeley girl, Jean Cox. He has never lived more than a few hundred yards from Mother and Father, both being allocated council housing at about the same time. George has always been Family to us.

When Mr. Owen got his second lorry, it was an ex army Dodge, very nice motor, painted in pleasant blue colour, with all the sign writing in gold. He employed Charlie Hamilton to be his driver when he came out of the navy.

The lorry was used for general work, but in the sugar-beet season it was in constant use for carting beet to Peterborough Sugar Factory.

When Charlie had a Saturday trip it was my good fortune to be able to go with him on occasions. At that time there was no loading equipment fitted to tractors like today. All the loading had to be done by hand with 'Beet Forks.' These were specially designed for the job and were very wide with long tines, with one tine each side raised above the others, making it almost shovel shaped. They were about 14 ins. Wide. The tines had round knobs on the ends about the size of marbles, to prevent the tines from piercing the beet and sticking on the fork.

On arriving at the factory you had to stop on the weigh bridge where a man would come along to check the paper work, and take a sample of beet off the lorry in a large bucket shaped vessel. This was taken to the Laboratory for testing, it involved washing all the soil off which was weighed against the washed beet to calculate the waste. It was also tested for sugar content. These tests determined the price paid to the farmer. If your lorry was of the tipping variety you just backed up to the large 'Flume' type pits and tipped your load in, after which you had to pass over the 'weigh bridge' again to determine the actual weight of your load.

Some Lorries were not 'tippers' including Charlie's, and the load had to be emptied by hand, which was more hard work. If the driver of these non tippers were lucky enough to have a special code on their paper work, they would be able to go under the washer. This meant driving up a slope straddling a pit, drop the tail board, and get back into the cab. The beet would be washed out of the lorry by a high pressure device operated by a man high up above the lorry.

It was very interesting to see all the different colours of soil that came in on the beet and trying to work out where they had come from. I knew the black soil very well, that came from the area of fens around Ramsey, Warboys and Chatteris. Then there were the red soils of various shades, they were from parts of Lincolnshire. Some of the black and reds had a high content of silver sand in, from the same areas but all slightly different. Then there was our own brownish gray with a lot of clay content These soils not only varied from area to area locally, but at times from field to field.

Sometimes we would bring home a load of sugar beet pulp, this was used for animal feed and was in large cube shaped sacks about three feet. square, they were dropped onto the lorry from a conveyer, still quite warm from the processing plant, and had to be stacked in a hurry as they came along at quite a rate. Sometimes you might not get out of the way soon enough, and one would fall on you, but they were very light, and so didn't hurt.

Vic Clarks Rabbits

When Vic Clark was our neighbour he bread and showed rabbits. He only kept 'Blue Beverans' this was a very large type. When fully grown they weighed about seven pounds. The ones that were not up to standard for showing were used to supplement the meat ration. They made very tasty eating, and a good meal for a large family. When they were prepared for the table Mr. Clark used to have the skins made into gloves for his daughters. They were a very nice blue/gray colour.

One skin made one full glove. Not the usual one, but more like a large gauntlet. The palms and fingers were of soft leather and the fur came right to the end of the fingers on the backs. So very warm.

Once when Mr. Clark and his family went away on holiday he left my Mother in charge of the rabbits, which she did willingly as she loved animals. Unfortunately on about the third day of caring for them, one of them died, Mother had thought that he looked 'a bit off colour' the day before, so it was a bit worrying for her. The next day another one died, so not knowing what to do, she sent for the vet, Mr. Hall from Huntingdon, he examined one or two of the others, but could not determine the problem. So he took one away for a post mortem. The outcome was that the rabbits were suffering from a disease known as Coccidiosis or spotted liver and would have died anyway, so no fault of Mothers, which was a little comforting for her, but she still dreaded telling Mr. Clark when he returned.

Places of Interest.

Like most villages, the Church is the centre of interest, no less so in Great Stukeley.

The Church is dedicated to Saint Bartholomew. Great Stukeley Church was mentioned in the Doomsday Survey of 1086. There are no remains of this early Church, which was most likely a timber structure, as the surrounding landscape would have been oak forest and at that time buildings were usually constructed with local materials.

Historians tell of a stone built Church in Norman times on this site, there are some Norman stones built into the walls of the current Church. They also suggest that Saint Bartholomew and Saint Martin at Little Stukeley were built partly from the stone of this Norman Church. And that the stone came from Barnac near Peterborough where stone was quarried for hundreds of years.

The current Church was built about 1250. It was extended early in the 14th century. In the 15th century two further extensions were carried out, one of which included the tower. This is built in the square, and it is reported that it is strong enough to have carried a spire. The tower houses four bells with various inscriptions and dates, 1626, 1635 and 1797. There are several local dignitaries buried within the Church, including some of the Torkington family of Great Stukeley Hall. There are also some of them buried in the church yard. When we were boys these graves had brick surrounds about two feet high with large flat slabs of stone on the tops, with all the information carved into them. Like massive grave stones, but laying flat. We used to try and look through the cracks in the brickwork, thinking we would see a skeleton.

In the history of Great Stukeley, The first time the family name Stukeley is mentioned was in 1346 then again in 1428. (But Little Stukeley history mentions the name as far back as the 11th century). In 1534 the Torkington family inherited the Hall and were in residence until 1901. In 1905 it was owned by the Coot family, (some of whom are also buried in the Church). In 1923 it was bought by Mr. Walter Fenwick, the family that I remember.

This the North side of St Bartolomew showing the North Door. This is used for the most occasions except funerals

There are two Roman burial mounds (Barrows) in the village, one on either side of Ermine Street, (a Roman road) One is just to the south side of the Council houses, and the other is in the corner of the sports field. When I was a lad and having no knowledge of ancient history, we were told that the one in the sports field was where Mr. Shelton had buried a horse, this was quite believable as there are a number of old graves in the church yard bearing the name Shelton

The Romans were possibly of high status being in Barrows, it was normal practice for the Romans to bury their dead at the road side, unmarked, and not being Christians they were buried at any angle, usually in the direction of the road.

There is another mound shown on the Ordnance Survey maps at the end of Green End. This I know to be of no significance with regard to ancient history, it was the spoil from the original manor house when it was built nearby. The mound is much smaller than when I first knew it. When I was a boy it was continually being dug off to make up the ground in the farm yard at Grange Farm. On the maps it shows an odd shape at one end, this is where my Father and the other men dug an opening so as to be able to reverse a trailer in for easier loading. This was carried out by hand, no diggers at that time! Once the top had been dug off and a flat surface emerged a tractor and plough was used to loosen the earth to make the digging easier.

The old rectory is of some interest although I am unable to put a date on it, I have been given to understand that it was started in the fourteenth century. At one time it was allegedly attacked by Cromwell's men and a cannon ball actually entered the house via a bedroom window. They were probably aiming at the church.

It is very different from when I was a boy. It has had several extensions and modifications, which have been very well done. I am told that in the very early days there was an office in part of the building where all the rents and tithes were paid by the strip farmers, and other tenants on the surrounding lands.

The old Post Office – possible now the oldest building in the village

At the top end of church road there is The Three Horseshoes Guest House & Restaurant. This is supposedly a Sixteenth Century coaching house. Coaching was a little before my time, I only remember it as a farm house.

In Owl End there are two interesting houses, both I think seventeenth century. One is College Farm. This has had to be virtually rebuilt, from below ground, and all the way up. The current owner tells me that he has been living here for thirteen years, and working on the restoration all the time. A large amount of all the old timbers have had to be replaced due to dilapidation and water intrusion, even some of the main beams have been restored, due to poor maintenance in the past.

All the timbers that have been replaced have been selected from reclamation yards, and have been dated as near as possible to the original. The gentleman showed me round the house when I explained to him about my story. What I have seen is a real credit to him; he deserves an award of some kind, for all the hard work that he has put into this project.

A true conservationist working on his own and I am sure a believer in our heritage.

The other house is Manor Farm although there is no farm now. I believe that this was the farm to the old manor house that was where Gt. Stukeley Hall stands.

This was the home of Professor Parker Smith. There have been no external alterations since I was a boy. But the current owner had no hesitation of showing me round the inside of the house, indicating all the restoration that he has already carried out, which has been done in a very sympathetic and caring manner, again keeping all the materials authentic. I would like to thank them both for their kindness in showing me over their homes. Neither of the gentlemen had any idea who I was when I first approached them.

At Green End, at Ermine Street end of the lane we still have the old blacksmiths shop, this has not changed in any way since I was a boy. All the old houses in this lane have been long gone, unfortunately. My old home and the houses opposite were 17th century, and at that time the only ones in Green End. (According to historical records.) I can't find any recorded dates of the present houses, but I am sure that the house where the Green family lived is the oldest in the lane now, the old Washingly Farm house being demolished some time ago, which would have been about the same age.

That just about brings my memories and observations up to school leaving age to a close. Some of my boyhood memories have carried on into later life, as the subjects were ongoing, like farming for instance. Others I have returned to recently, to see what has been going on. There is a long gap between eight to fifteen years of age, and then onto present age, seventy five.

I think I have mentioned all the people of Gt. Stukeley living there when I was about six to ten years of age. After that time people started to move around, and it is easy to lose track. I apologize for any I may have missed, and also for any I may have offended.

I now have to try to get my story published, if you are reading this, then I have been successful. If I have been, then I owe a great deal of thanks to the lovely Margaret Faulkner. For all the encouragement and advice she gave me, as without her I might never have started it. Also for being my proof reader, keeping me on the right track, and making my story legible.

Margaret and I go back a long way, we were childhood sweethearts at about the age of ten. She was a lovely girl then, and still is.